HEINEMANN • ENGLISH • LAN



# H·E·L·P WITH GRAMMAR 2

SUE LAVENDER
WILL FORSYTH

HEINEMANN

Heinemann English Language Practice Series

Titles in this series include:

| | | | |
|---|---|---|---|
| **Help with Grammar 1** | Will Forsyth, Sue Lavender | | 0 435 28118 6 |
| **Help with Grammar 2** | Will Forsyth, Sue Lavender | | 0 435 28119 4 |
| **Help with Idioms** | Jane Applebee, Anton Rush | | 0 435 28116 X |
| **Help with Phrasal Verbs** | Richard Acklam | (book) | 0 435 28114 3 |
| | | (cassette) | 0 435 28115 1 |
| **Help with Words** | Nick Hall, John Shepheard | | 0 435 28117 8 |

Heinemann English Language Teaching
A division of Heinemann Publishers (Oxford) Ltd
Halley Court, Jordan Hill, Oxford OX2 8EJ

OXFORD MADRID ATHENS PARIS FLORENCE PRAGUE
SÃO PAULO CHICAGO MELBOURNE AUCKLAND SINGAPORE TOKYO
GABORONE JOHANNESBURG PORTSMOUTH (NH) IBADAN

ISBN 0 435 28119 4


First published 1994

*For John Lavender, to remember you always*



Designed by Helen Hible
Illustrations by Belinda Evans, Satoshi Kambayashi, Mike Mosedale, Shaun Williams

Typeset in 11/13 pt Sabon and 10/12 pt Helvetica

Printed and bound in Great Britain by The Bath Press, Avon

94 95 96 97 98 10 9 8 7 6 5 4 3 2 1

# Contents

Page

# Notes to the student

**Help with Grammar 2** is designed to improve your understanding of important grammar points, and to help you use them correctly. You will find it useful if you are an upper-intermediate level student, or if you are beginning a course for the Cambridge First Certificate Examination.

HOW TO USE THE BOOK
**Help with Grammar 2** is easy to use without a teacher. The units are arranged from easy to more difficult, so you can work through the book from beginning to end if you wish to do so. If you are more interested in a single grammar point you can use the *Contents* page or the *Index* to select all the exercises on that one point. There are also references at the end of each unit to other units which deal with similar language.

There is a wide variety of exercises. Many of them are based on pictures or situations which show you exactly when the structures are used. There is a theme running through a lot of the units to make them more interesting.

Many of the units have special sections called *Can you work it out?* which encourage you to think about the grammar rules for yourself. For example, you can work out when to use forms like *I got used to living in a small house,* how to form structures such as *Could you tell me when the first bus is?*, or the difference between *so* and *such.*

***Which are my weak areas?***
If you are not sure which areas you need to study, turn to the *Checking ahead* units (units 1, 25) which test your understanding of some of the structures in the following units. You can use these units to decide which areas you need to concentrate on.

***Checking your progress***
You can check the progress you have made by doing the units called *Getting it right* (units 17, 37, 51) which test your understanding and knowledge of points which have already been covered in the previous units.

# Notes to the teacher

**Help with Grammar 2** is for students at an upper-intermediate level, including those preparing for the Cambridge First Certificate Examination. It deals with grammatical structures which appear in most coursebooks but which learners still have regular trouble understanding and using.

**Help with Grammar 2** can be used in the presentation, practice or revision of structures.

DIAGNOSIS
The *Checking ahead* units (units 1, 25) provide a quick test of some of the structures in the units which follow them and can be used to check on learners' weaknesses in those areas.

PRESENTATION
As part of a presentation of new language, the situations in **Help with Grammar** can be used to bring the structure alive. You can present the situation to the class by, for example, telling the story of John in *Wish 1* (unit 18). The learners can offer their own way of telling the story, and you can encourage the correct use of the target structure. The oral introduction livens the lesson up and allows the teacher to check pronunciation and response speed (both important factors in conversation). After this, the learners can write the exercise in the book, working either individually, or discussing it in pairs or groups. It is useful to discuss the answers together afterwards, as this helps the learners work out what is correct and why.

PRACTICE
After the initial presentation, many exercises can be developed to allow the learners to use the target structure in freer and more natural language practice. For example, in *Prepositions 2* (unit 43), after Part A, students can be presented with more objects and asked to define their use and in part B students can ask each other to define other objects and places. Where there are picture situations, as in *Modal verbs 1* (unit 7), similar sentences can be given to the learners, who can then make up situations which include the given structures.

The units in the book can be used as short activities at the beginning or end of a lesson, or given for homework. Many exercises can be extended orally and in written form, for example, after completing the unit on *The past* (unit 45) learners can be encouraged to bring in photographs to talk about their own pasts and then write about these for homework.

THEORY
The *Can you work it out?* activities are entertaining as puzzles and should be used as such, with plenty of discussion. They should not be used to introduce the structures. This is because the exercises either contrast two or more frequently confused forms (for example, different ways of talking about the future) or show the mechanics of complex grammatical forms (for example, indirect speech or the passive). Instead, when the learners have already met the structures, the exercises can be used as the basis for discussion either by the class and teacher together or by the learners in groups.

REVISION
There are test units called *Getting it right* (units 17, 37, 51) which can be given to the class to check that the learners understand and remember the points covered in the previous units, if you are working through the book together.

We hope you enjoy using this book and that it gives you ideas for exercises of your own.

# Checking ahead 1

1

**Here are some structures dealt with in units 2 to 24. Match each sentence with the correct picture, *a* or *b*.**

a

**Example:**
She used to cycle up the hill.

She's used to cycling up the hill.

b

a

1 What eats birds?

2 What do birds eat?

b

a

3 There are plenty of seats.

4 There are enough seats.

b

a

5 She's seeing the mayor.

6 She can see the mayor.

b

a

7 You could drown!

8 You could have drowned!

b

Also see unit 25

# 2 Countable and uncountable 1

**Use the words in bold to finish each of the three sentences. Be careful: sometimes you have to use *a*, for example *a time*, sometimes you have to make the word plural, for example, *times* and sometimes you have to leave the word as it is, for example *time*.**

**time**

**Example:**

Has there ever been _a time_ when you've felt happy for no reason at all?

1 Learning anything well takes ___________ .

2 There will often be ___________ when you don't know what to do.

**glass**

3 Windows are made of ___________ .

4 Would you like ___________ of wine?

5 Do you wear ___________ ?

**light**

6 They left ___________ on all over the house, but they were still burgled.

7 I've got a cigarette, but I haven't got ___________ .

8 ___________ travels at about 300 000 km a second.

**hope**

9 They lost everything except ___________ .

10 It was something he had always wanted, but it was ___________ he never realised.

11 Different people have different ___________ for themselves and their children.

**lamb**

12 We saw ___________ playing with one another in the fields.

13 He's as gentle as ___________ .

14 We sell ___________ at £2.00 a kilo.

# Can you work it out?

**A Match each sentence with one of the two pictures, *a* or *b*.**

1 'Mummy, can I have a lamb?'

2 'Mummy, can I have some lamb?'

3 'Would you like some more cake?'

4 'Would you like another cake?'

5 'It's technically perfect, but it doesn't have any emotion.'

6 'It's very intelligent, but it doesn't have any emotions.'

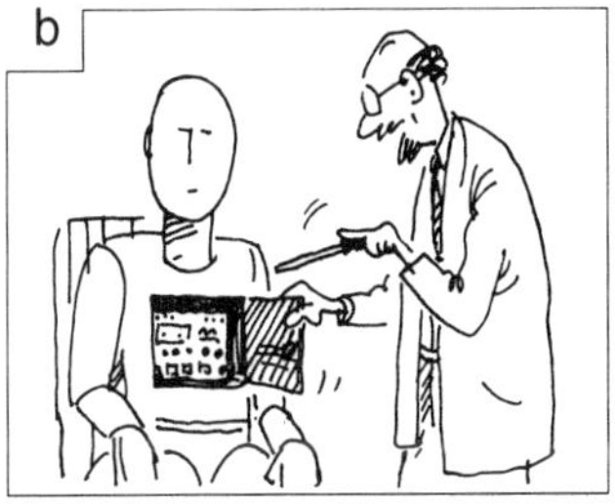

**B Some nouns are only countable, for example, *picture* and *oats*. Some nouns are only uncountable, for example *music* and *wheat*. But many nouns can be either countable or uncountable, depending on the meaning. Match the meanings, forms and examples then finish the example with the correct form of *hair*.**

| Meaning | Form | Example |
|---|---|---|
| **Example:** The material that something is made of | a) The singular form, for example, *a hair* | i) The detective found three ____________ on his shirt. |
| 1 Whole individual items | b) The uncountable form, for example, *hair* | ii) Hairdressers cut and style ____________ . |
| 2 A whole, individual item | c) The plural form, for example, *hairs* | iii) Wigs are made of hair ____________ . |
| 3 Something thought of as a mass, not individual items | d) The uncountable form, for example, *hair* | iv) I'm coughing because I've got ____________ in my throat. |

Also see units 30, 48

# 3 Subject and object questions

A Here is part of a leaflet about a new film 'Murder at Midnight'. Unfortunately, the leaflet has been torn and part is missing. Complete the questions you need to ask to find out the missing information about the new film.

**MURDER AT MIDNIGHT – COMING SOON**

**Starring Martin Symes as**
**Directed by**
**Produced by**
**Filmed on location in**
**Musical score by**

**This film has won**
**'Time Out' says**
**Opens in London on**

Example:
Who *does Martin Symes* ____ star as?
1 Who ____ the film?
2 Who ____ the film?
3 Where ____ filmed?
4 Who ____ the musical score?
5 What ____ the film won?
6 What ____ say?
7 When ____ in London?

B Here is a review of the film 'Murder at Midnight'.

MURDER AT MIDNIGHT: based on the popular Detective Clithero novel by A J Smith
One night, the butler discovered the body of Lord Mayhew in his study. He had been mysteriously poisoned by wine. The following day, the butler saw a strange figure, then the butler too was attacked …
All is solved by Detective Clithero. This is a film you MUST see!

**Make questions to the answers using the words in the box.**

| | | |
|---|---|---|
| What<br>Who | did<br>– | the butler find?<br>the butler see?<br>poisoned Lord Mayhew?<br>solved the crime?<br>wrote the novel? |

Example: *What did the butler find* ____? Lord Mayhew's body.
1 ____? The wine.
2 ____? A strange figure.
3 ____? Detective Clithero.
4 ____? A J Smith.

# Can you work it out?

**A Match each question with the correct picture, *a* or *b*.**

a

1 How many plates broke?

2 How many plates did they break?

b

a

3 What crashed into you?

4 What did you crash into?

b

**B Decide which question, *a* or *b*, the statements refer to.**

a) Who taught Einstein?
b) Who did Einstein teach?

1 *Who* refers to the teacher. ____________

2 *Who* refers to the pupils. ____________

3 *Who* is the subject of the verb *teach.* ____________

4 *Who* is the object of the verb *teach.* ____________

a) What did the discovery lead to?
b) What led to the discovery?

5 *What* refers to the cause of the *discovery.* ____________

6 *What* refers to the result of the *discovery.* ____________

7 *What* is the subject of the verb *lead.* ____________

8 *What* is the object of the verb *lead.* ____________

**C Megan teaches in a primary school. Here are some answers the children in her class have given her. Use the verb in bold to write the question Megan asked them.**

**Example:** Columbus **discovered** America. Who discovered America ?

1 Shakespeare **wrote** Hamlet. Who ____________ ?

2 The Americans **landed** on the moon in 1969. Who ____________ ?

3 Light **travels** at 300 000 km per second. How fast ____________ ?

4 The phone was **invented** by Bell. Who ____________ ?

5 Canada and Mexico **border** the USA. Which countries ____________ ?

6 Wren **designed** St Paul's Cathedral. Who ____________ ?

7 The moon **causes** the sea level to change. What ____________ ?

8 Neil Armstrong **said,** 'One small step for a man, one giant step for mankind'. What ____________ ?

Also see units 9, 36, 39, 47

# 4 Adverbs of time 1

**A friend asks you some questions. Read your thoughts and then answer your friend using the word given in brackets.**

| What your friend asks: | Your thoughts: | What you say: |
|---|---|---|
| **Example:** Would you like to see 'Dusty Moonlight'? | You saw it last night. | Actually, I've already seen it. (already) |
| 1 Did you enjoy the book I lent you? | The book is unread. | I'm afraid ______ ______ (yet) |
| 2 Have you rung Jane? | You know you promised to do this last week but there hasn't been time. | I'm sorry but ______ ______ (still) |
| 3 How long have you had that shirt? | You bought it when you went to India. | I've ______ ______ (since) |
| 4 Do you know Steve's coming round this evening? | This will be the first time you've met him. | I don't think I ______ ______ (ever) |
| 5 Would you like to borrow this novel? | You've read it before. | Thanks, but to tell you the truth I've ______ ______ (already) |
| 6 Shall we go to an Indian restaurant tonight? | It will be your first visit to an Indian restaurant. | That'll be exciting, I ______ (never) |
| 7 Have I seen that hat before? | You got it six months ago. | Yes, I think so, I ______ ______ (for) |
| 8 How do you think I can do all this garden on my own? | You think it would be a good idea to employ a gardener. | Have you ______ ______ (ever)? |

# Can you work it out?

**A Rewrite the following sentences to include the word in brackets.**

**Example:**
I haven't been to Australia. (ever) *I haven't ever been to Australia.*

1 I've been to Australia. (already) ______

2 I haven't been to Australia. (yet) ______

3 Have you been to Australia? (ever) ______

4 I've been to Australia. (never) ______

5 I haven't been to Australia. (still) ______

6 Australia is the most beautiful country I've seen. (ever) ______

**B Here are some possible continuations of the sentences in A. Write the letter of the most appropriate continuation next to the number of each sentence.**

**Example:** *b* 1 ______ 2 ______ 3 ______ 4 ______ 5 ______ 6 ______

a) so I strongly recommend it for a holiday.

b) and I have no special plans to go there.

c) so I'd like to go somewhere different this year.

d) I can't remember if you've told me.

e) and I have no special plans to go there.

f) but I hope to go one day soon.

g) although I've been trying to go for a long time.

**C Choose the *most appropriate* word to add to each sentence and then write the sentence with the word in the correct place.**

**Example:**
I've been to Paris; I was there last year. yet/already
*I've already been to Paris; I was there last year.*

1 It's the most beautiful picture I've seen. never/ever

______

2 I haven't been to Germany, but I'd like to go one day. never/ever

______

3 You were talking about going to Munich; have you been there? ever/yet

______

4 I'm trying to find someone who knows about Canada; have you been there? ever/yet

______

5 Although Mongolia has opened its borders, it's difficult to fly there. still/yet

______

Also see units 26, 46

# 5 Prepositions 1

**A You are interviewing Peter Schanks, world tennis champion. Fill in the missing prepositions and then put the answers in the puzzle to find the hidden word.**

**Example:** When did you arrive _in_ this country?

1 And how long are you planning to stay here ____ ?
2 Are you looking forward ____ the championship?
3 Are you afraid ____ losing your title this year, Peter?
4 What do you feel your success has been due ____ ?
5 Do you believe ____ training every day?
6 How many of this year's competitions will you be involved ____ ?
7 And which competition are you most interested ____ winning?
8 What type of tennis do you think you're best ____ ?
9 Who did you pick up most of your techniques ____ ?
10 Finally, Peter, are you fond ____ other types of sport?

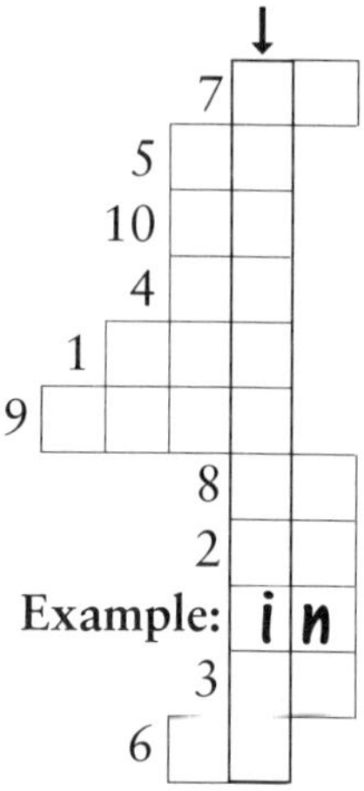


**B Match each expression with the correct preposition to find out what sorts of people Alice likes and dislikes.**

**Expressions**

take advantage ____ other people.
can't take pleasure ____ simple things.
disagree ____ me sometimes, but not always.
I can depend ____ .
remember people ____ name.
never criticise you ____ your back.
need to have a reason ____ everything.
are enthusiastic ____ what they are doing.
frequently get ____ control.
laugh ____ other people's misfortunes.

**I like people who ...**

**Example:** about: _are enthusiastic about what they are doing._

1 on: ________________

2 by: ________________

3 behind: ________________

4 with: ________________

**I don't like people who ...**

5 of: ________________

6 for: ________________

7 out of: ________________

8 in: ________________

9 at: ________________

Also see unit 43

# Enough and plenty

# 6

The Hubert family, two adults and four children, want to rent a house in Britain for the summer. They have just visited a house and the estate agent has given them a list of items in the kitchen. Unfortunately, the number of items is not always appropriate. Using the phrases in the box, write the family's comments in the correct place on the list.

| | | |
|---|---|---|
| (there aren't enough) | there are plenty | there isn't enough |
| just the right amount | there is plenty | just the right number |
| there isn't enough | this isn't big enough | these aren't big enough |
| there aren't quite enough | there are far too many | there aren't enough |

**KITCHEN INVENTORY**

Example: *there aren't enough* — Glasses: 6 large glasses, 3 small glasses

1 ______ — Crockery: 6 dishes, 6 plates (large), 6 plates (small), 6 cups, 6 saucers

Cutlery: 6 knives, 6 forks, 5 spoons — 2 ______, 4 serving spoons

3 ______ — Cooking equipment: 1 small saucepan, 1 small frying pan

Linen: 10 hand towels — 4 ______, 2 tea-towels — 5 ______, 6 napkins — 6 ______

7 ______ — Furniture: 2 chairs, 1 small kitchen table — 8 ______

9 ______ — Appliances: 1 small fridge, 1 small freezer

1 cooker, 1 dish-washer

10 ______ — Storage space: 8 large shelves, 6 large cupboards

1 side-board

Other: 42 house plants (please water!) — 11 ______

# 7 Modal verbs 1

**Look at the pictures and complete what each person is saying using a verb from the box. Sometimes more than one verb is possible.**

| would | should | could | might |
|---|---|---|---|

**Example:**

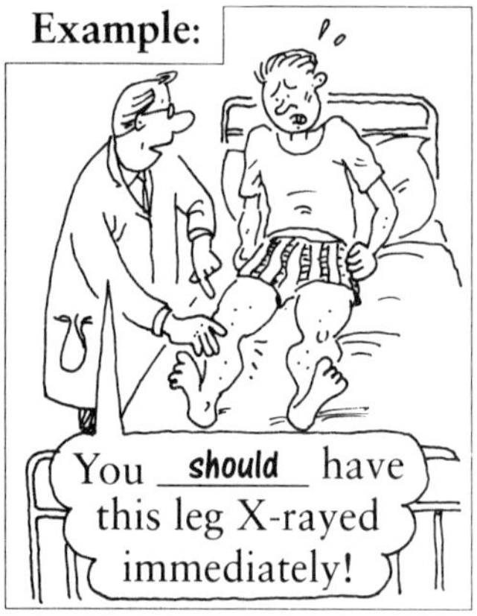


1

2

3

4

5

6

7

8

# Can you work it out?

**A Match the beginning of each sentence with the most appropriate ending, *a* or *b*.**

| | |
|---|---|
| 1 You should wear a seat belt | a) if you drive in Britain. |
| 2 You would wear a seat belt | b) if you drove in Britain. |
| 3 If you applied for that job you would get it; | a) but I don't really think you'd have very much chance. |
| 4 If you applied for that job you might/could get it | b) with your qualifications they'd be certain to take you. |
| 5 It should be even warmer tomorrow; | a) but I really hope not. |
| 6 It might/could be even warmer tomorrow | b) it said so on the forecast. |
| 7 She could play the piano as a child | a) but now she's forgotten how to. |
| 8 She would play the piano as a child | b) whenever guests came. |
| 9 You could see a doctor about that | a) I'm positive it needs medical attention. |
| 10 You should see a doctor about that; | b) but I don't think it's really necessary. |

**B Match the meanings below with the numbers of the sentences from part A. Note that some of the meanings match more than one sentence.**

a) an ability someone had in the past ______
b) a habit someone had in the past ______
c) the certain outcome of an 'if' clause __2__ and ______
d) the possible outcome of an 'if' clause ______
e) strong advice for someone to do something __1__ and ______
f) a good outcome in the future based on strong evidence ______
g) the possibility that something will happen in the future ______
h) a suggestion for someone to do something ______

**C Complete the sentence using a word from the box.**

| would | should | could | might |
|---|---|---|---|

**Example:** If you want someone to do something you ask if they __would__ or __could__ do it for you.

1 If you have strong evidence that something good will happen in the future you say it ______ happen.
2 If you think it's possible that something will happen in the future you say it ______ or ______ happen.
3 If you want to give someone strong advice you say they ______ do something.
4 If you want to make a suggestion you say someone ______ do something.
5 If you are talking about an ability in the past you say someone ______ do something.
6 If you are talking about a habit in the past you say someone ______ do something.
7 To talk about the certain outcome of an 'if' clause you use ______ .
8 To talk about the possible outcome of an 'if' clause you use ______ or ______ .

Also see units 11, 19, 20, 29, 34

# 8 So and such

## A Complete the sentences with *so* or *such*.

I went to Spain last year and I enjoyed it __so__ much that I want to go back. I had 1 ____ beautiful weather that I stayed outdoors all the time and the sea was 2 ____ warm that I never wanted to get out. The shops were selling 3 ____ wonderful cheap leather that I bought presents for all my friends. The people I met were 4 ____ friendly – they were always inviting me to their homes. I did 5 ____ many interesting things I can't even remember them all.

## B Ferhan is visiting England. It is very different from her own country. Complete the sentences with phrases using *so* or *such* and the opposite of the word in *italics*.

**Example:** She thinks the city is *boring* because she comes __from such an interesting city.__

1 She thinks the weather is *cold* because in her country it's ____________________

____________________________________________

2 She thinks the house is *small* because she has ____________________

3 She thinks there's very *little* to do here because in her own city there's

____________________________________________

4 She thinks the people drive *well* because the people in her own country

____________________________________________

5 She thinks English families are *small* because she has ____________________

6 She thinks they have *short* names because in her country everyone's name is

____________________________________________

7 She thinks the food is *bad* because they have ____________________

8 She thinks there are very *few* children in the streets because in her country there ____________________

## C Write out these thoughts in complete sentences, using *so* or *such* before the word(s) in *italics* each time. Do not change the order of words given.

**Example:** wind *strong* – nearly blew bike over — __The wind was so strong that it nearly blew my bike over.__

1 *dark night* – couldn't see path in front of me ____________________

2 then saw crowd of people; *many* – couldn't count them ____________________

3 they were all glowing with *bright light* – lit the path ahead ____________________

4 I going *fast* – couldn't stop ____________________

5 but suddenly vanished; I never *scared* – in life before ____________________

# Can you work it out?

**A Read these sentences and put the phrases in *italics* into the correct box.**

| Noun phrases, a lot, a few, a little | Adjectives, adverbs, much, many, few, little |
|---|---|
| such a kind man | |
| | |
| | |
| | |
| | |
| | |

**Example:**

What I like about Peter is that he's *such a kind man.*

1 What I like about Peter is that he's *so kind.*

2 It was *so cold* that I didn't go out.

3 He was *so good* at mathematics that he went to university when he was 16 years old.

4 There are *such a lot of people* here that we'll never find him.

5 I've never tasted *such delicious fruit* as I did in Singapore.

6 They drove away *so fast* that no one could catch them.

7 Thank you for giving me *so much* of your time.

8 He was *such a little boy* when he was 10 that everyone thought he was younger.

9 They're *such interesting people* that it's strange they have *so few* friends.

**B Decide whether these sentences are correct. Put a tick ✓ in the box if the sentence is right and a cross ✗ if it is not. Correct the sentences with mistakes.**

1 I've never met anyone such interesting before. ☐ ____________________

2 Italy is so beautiful country that I never want to live anywhere else. ☐ ____________________

3 There was so little food that everyone still felt hungry after the meal. ☐ ____________________

4 I met so nice man last weekend. ☐ ____________________

5 I've never eaten so nice food before. ☐ ____________________

# 9 Indirect questions

**A You are staying with your friend, Liz. One morning Liz leaves you the following note.**

> Hi! I'm afraid I'm in a panic. The Dumals, (the French family I worked for last year), have just rung to say that they're coming this weekend. If you have time today, could you make the following phone calls for me?
>
> | | |
> |---|---|
> | Bus station | time of first bus to Heathrow on Friday morning. |
> | Heathrow airport | arrival time for BA 272. |
> | Bargain Car Hire | cost of car hire for 2 days. |
> | Hill Guest House | double room available this weekend? |
> | Train station | cost of family day excursion ticket to London. |
> | Hong Hu Restaurant | open on Sunday evenings? |
> | Diana | come and meet them on Sunday? |
>
> Thanks a lot - you'll find all the numbers in my address book. **Liz**

**Now finish the questions you need to ask each person you ring.**

**Example: Bristol Bus Station** Could you tell me what time *the first bus to Heathrow on Friday morning is*?

1 **Bristol Station** Could you tell me how much ________________________ ?

2 **Hill Guest House** I'd like to know ________________________ ?

3 **Bargain Car Hire** A friend of mine would like to know how much ________________________ ?

4 **Heathrow** I wonder if you can tell me what time ________________________ ?

5 **Hong Hu** Could you tell me ________________________ ?

6 **Diana** Liz wants to know whether ________________________ ?

**B Here are some things the Dumals need to know. Complete the sentences by choosing a phrase or item from each box.**

| if what time how long whether (how far) |  | . ? |
|---|---|---|

**Example:** I'd like to know *how far* away the station is *.*

1 Could you tell us ________ the next bus arrives ____

2 Do you happen to know ________ or not the chemist is open late ____

3 Have you any idea ________ there's a market near here ____

4 We'd like to know ________ the flight takes ____

# Can you work it out?

**A In these two conversations David is talking on the phone to a shop-assistant and to a friend, Rita, about a new computer he wants to buy. Put the questions from the box into the correct conversation.**

a) Do you happen to know which is the nearest bus stop for your shop?
b) Is that before or after tax?
c) And how much are they?
d) I don't suppose you remember how much your Roplex was?
e) Could you tell me if you have any Roplex XT1000Es in stock?

1 **David:** ______________________________?
**Shop assistant:** Yes, plenty.
**David:** ______________________________?
**Shop assistant:** £985 excluding tax.
**David:** ______________________________?
**Shop assistant:** Yes, Oxford Circus.

2 **David:** ______________________________?
**Rita:** About £1000, but it's difficult to remember.
**David:** ______________________________?
**Rita:** Before, I'm afraid.

**B Both of the conversations begin with indirect questions. Which of the following do you think are true about the use of indirect questions? Put a tick ✓ next to the ones which are true and a cross ✗ by any which are not.**

1 You often use indirect questions to begin a conversation with someone you don't know well. ☐

2 Once you have begun a conversation with an indirect question it's normal to ask other questions in the same way. ☐

3 You often use indirect questions when you think your question is unusual or that someone might not know the answer. ☐

**C David is talking to a passenger he has never met before at the bus stop. Change any questions *you think necessary* in the following conversation into indirect questions. Begin with 'Do you happen to know ...' each time.**

**David:** What time's the next bus due?

1 ______________________________

**Passenger:** In about five minutes I think.
**David:** Great, not long, then. Does it go to Oxford Circus?

2 ______________________________

**Passenger:** I hope so, that's where I'm going!
**David:** Oh, where's the Comsoft computer shop?

3 ______________________________

**Passenger:** Never heard of it, I'm afraid.

Also see units 3, 36, 39, 47

# 10 Advice

**A Your friend Richa is giving you some advice about your stay in Britain. Write her suggestions using a phrase from each box each time.**

| | | |
|---|---|---|
| Maybe you should<br>Why don't you<br>I think you'd better<br>How about<br>If I were you I'd<br>You could always<br>Have you thought<br>Why not<br>Perhaps you ought | visiting Wales<br>of staying in a bed and breakfast<br>rent a car<br>to come and stay with me | .<br>? |

Example: Maybe you should rent a car.

1 ______
2 ______
3 ______
4 ______
5 ______
6 ______
7 ______
8 ______

**B Richa is telling you about some problems she has. Complete your advice to her by choosing the appropriate picture and using the verb given.**

buy

look

have

take

use

| **Richa's problem** | **Your advice** |
|---|---|
| **Example:** I have a bad headache today. | Perhaps you should take some asprin. |
| 1 The bus is really expensive! | Well, have you thought ______ |
| 2 This cassette player sounds terrible! | Why not ______ |
| 3 I find it really difficult to see the TV. | Maybe you ought ______ |
| 4 There are so many words in this book that I don't know! | Well, you could always ______ |

# Can you work it out?

**A Look at the pictures and comments and choose the most appropriate reply, *a* or *b*.**

1

a) You ought to be wearing a seat belt.
b) If I were you, I'd be wearing a seat belt.

2

a) Yes, you could always have it out today.
b) Yes, you'd better have it out today.

3

a) You'd better try painting it green.
b) Why don't you try painting it green?

4

a) Quick, you'd better get a cloth!
b) Quick, have you thought of getting a cloth?

5

a) You should get it repaired over there.
b) How about getting it repaired over there?

6

a) Yes, why not take the medicine twice a day before meals?
b) Yes, you should take the medicine twice a day before meals.

**B Match the correct replies in A with their meanings. Note that a reply may match more than one meaning.**

a) The speaker is giving professional advice. __1a__ ____ ____
b) The speaker is giving advice as a friend or equal. ____ ____ ____
c) The speaker is suggesting only one of a number of possible courses of action. ____ ____
d) The speaker is strongly suggesting one immediate action as the only possibility. ____ ____

Also see units 27, 28, 44

# 11 Modal verbs 2

**A Jerry Lindsay is going to Guatemala for a year. His mother is worried about the trip. Write her questions using *will have to* or *will be able to* and a word or phrase from the box.**

| |
|---|
| come home go camping learn (phone) have find a job drive a car write |

**Example:** Will you be able to phone ______ us?
Oh yes; it's possible to dial direct from there.

1 **Mother:** ______ there?
**Jerry:** Not at first, I've saved enough money to last for a few months.

2 **Mother:** ______ Spanish while you're there?
**Jerry:** Yes; not many people speak English there, but I want to anyway.

3 **Mother:** ______ in the countryside?
**Jerry:** I certainly hope so; that's one of the reasons I want to go.

4 **Mother:** ______ to you?
**Jerry:** Oh yes. I'll send you my address as soon as I can.

5 **Mother:** ______ there?
**Jerry:** I think so; I've got an international driving licence.

6 **Mother:** ______ lots of injections?
**Jerry:** I've already had them.

7 **Mother:** ______ if you really want to?
**Jerry:** Yes, of course I will; I've always got my return ticket.

**B A reporter is interviewing a student about politics. Complete the sentences with *can, must, be able to* or *have to* in the correct form and the verb in brackets. Sometimes you need to use *will*.**

**Reporter:** Can I ask ______ you a few questions about politics in your country?
**Student:** Yes, certainly.
**Reporter:** How old 1 ______ (be) to vote in your country?
**Student:** Eighteen; my age. I'm just eighteen.
**Reporter:** So you 2 ______ (vote) at the next election.
**Student:** That's right; for the first time.
**Reporter:** Do you know who you're going to vote for?
**Student:** I'm not sure. If the national party wins we 3 ______ (start) doing national service and they'll cut spending on education so a lot of people 4 ______ (not go) to university, but at the same time we 5 ______ (not pay) so much tax.
**Reporter:** Are most people very interested in politics in your country?
**Student:** Oh yes, a lot of people think we 6 ______ (keep) the national party out at all costs and get the social party in.
**Reporter:** Do you think they 7 ______ (do) that?
**Student:** I don't know. We 8 ______ (see).

# Can you work it out?

**A In the following dialogues put a tick in the box if the sentences are possible. Sometimes only one sentence is possible, but sometimes both *a* and *b* are possible.**

**Example:**

We're going to Ulaan Baatar next month;
- a) can we telephone direct from there? ☑
- b) will we be able to telephone direct from there? ☑

1 They're putting in an international phone line next month;
- a) can we telephone direct then? ☐
- b) will we be able to telephone direct then? ☐

2 My legs are badly broken, aren't they, doctor?
- a) Yes, but you can walk again in eight months or so. ☐
- b) Yes, you'll be able to walk again in eight months or so. ☐

3 I feel much better now, doctor.
- a) Yes, you can leave at the end of the week. ☐
- b) Yes, you'll be able to leave at the end of the week. ☐

4 We don't have to study foreign languages at the moment, but Mrs Vine becomes head teacher next year
- a) and then we have to study French or German. ☐
- b) and then we'll have to study French or German. ☐

5 When you go to senior school
- a) you have to study French or German. ☐
- b) you'll have to study French or German. ☐

6 You can start tomorrow if you like
- a) but you must arrive as early as you can. ☐
- b) but you'll have to arrive as early as you can. ☐

7 You don't have to pay much tax now, but if the conservatives are elected
- a) you have to pay even less. ☐
- b) you'll have to pay even less. ☐

**B Match each sentence beginning with its correct ending.**

1 You use *can* to say that

2 You use *will be able to* to say that

3 You use *must* or *have to* to say that

4 You use *will have to* to say that

a) it is not yet possible (but it will be).

b) it is possible now (to do it now or in the future).

c) it is necessary now (to do it now or in the future).

d) it is not necessary yet (but it will be).

Also see units 7, 19, 20, 29, 34

# 12 Senses and actions

**Read the questions and complete the answers using a verb from the box. Be careful; sometimes you have to use:**

| | |
|---|---|
| can/could | (for example, I can feel/I could feel) |
| am/was -ing | (for example, I'm feeling/I was feeling) |
| present or past simple | (for example, I feel/I felt) |

| | | | | |
|---|---|---|---|---|
| feel | smell | taste | hear/listen to | see/look at |

**Example:**

Why did that man open ten bottles of wine and then only drink a little of each one?
(He/it) He was tasting it.

1 Don't eat that; it's for the guests!
(Don't worry, I/only/it) ____________

2 What's in this ice cream?
(I don't know, but I/honey and nuts) ____________

3 How do you know the letter's from his girlfriend?
(It/of perfume) ____________

4 Why are you holding your nose up like that?
(I/this wonderful sea air) ____________

5 How do you know there was someone next door?
(I/voices, but they've stopped now) ____________

6 Why don't you talk to me?
(Please be quiet, I/the music) ____________

7 Do you know someone called Helen Sharman?
(Yes, in fact I/her tomorrow) ____________

8 Do you think she'll come?
(Yes. In fact I/her coming now; look) ____________

9 Why did you stop?
(I/that church; it's really beautiful) ____________

10 What's wrong? You're shaking.
(I/really cold) ____________

11 Why have you got your hand in the water?
(I/the temperature) ____________

12 What's that? Is it an earthquake?
(I/not/anything) ____________

13 What is it?
(You/a ship over there?) ____________

14 He's blind.
(I don't think so; I think he/) ____________

15 It's nice here; there's no one else for miles.
(I think there is; I/a radio) ____________

# Can you work it out?

**A Match each sentence with one of the two pictures.**

a

1 He's seeing the president.
2 He can see the president.

b

a

3 I can taste coconut.
4 I was tasting the coconut.

b

a

5 I could hear music.
6 I was listening to music.

b

a

7 I can smell perfume.
8 I'm smelling the perfume.

b

**B Write the numbers of the sentences from part A in the correct sentence.**

1 Sentences 1_______, _______, _______ and _______ describe *actions.*
2 Sentences _______, _______, _______ and _______ describe *feelings* or *senses.*

**C Choose the correct ending to each sentence, *a* or *b*.**

1 'What's the matter?' a) 'I thought I saw something move out there.'
b) 'I thought I looked at something move out there.'

2 He sat in front of the picture for 20 minutes; a) he was seeing it.
b) he was looking at it.

3 If it's something you feel or sense, you usually say a) 'I can taste/feel/smell it.'
b) 'I'm tasting/feeling/smelling it.'

4 If it's an action, you usually say a) 'I can taste/feel/smell it.'
b) 'I'm tasting/feeling/smelling it.'

5 *See* and *hear* are usually a) senses.
b) actions.

6 *Look* and *listen* are a) senses.
b) actions.

# 13 Present perfect and past simple

**Look at the pictures and complete what each of the people is saying. Use a verb from the box in the correct form. (You need to use some verbs twice.)**

| forget | break | go | spill | ski | (hit) | drive | be | land |
|---|---|---|---|---|---|---|---|---|

**Example:**

Ouch! I've hit my head!

1

Drat! I ______________ ______________ my wine!

2

I ______________ to Australia in 1982.

3

Oh dear! ______________ the phone number!

4

In 1969, they ______________ ______________ on the moon.

5

Ouch! ______________ ______________ my leg!

6

Mrs Thatcher ______________ ______________ Prime Minister from 1979 to 1990.

7

This is the first time I ______________ since my driving test!

8

I'm afraid I ______________ ______________ before!

# Can you work it out?

**A Match the beginning of each sentence with its correct ending, *a* or *b*.**

1 I've lost my key
2 I lost my key

a) so I couldn't get in.
b) so I can't get in.

3 I changed my mind
4 I've changed my mind

a) so I didn't go.
b) so I'm not going.

5 I lived here for five years;
6 I've lived here for five years;

a) and I really like it.
b) and I really liked it.

7 I did that report
8 I've done that report

a) sometime last week.
b) so I'll put it on your desk today.

9 I never met Carol;
10 I've never met Carol;

a) I hope I have the chance to.
b) I wish I'd had the chance to.

11 Ever thought of going to Scotland;
12 Did you think of going to Scotland

a) it's really nice, you know?
b) when you had your holiday in Europe?

**B Write *present perfect* or *past simple* in the correct sentences.**

**Example:**
When the action has an effect now or in the future you use the *present perfect.*

1 When you want to begin a conversation on a new subject without mentioning a definite time you often use ____________

2 When you are talking about a definite finished time in the past you use ____________

3 When both an action and its results are finished you normally use ____________

4 When you are talking about people who are dead you normally use ____________

5 When you are talking about experiences in the lives of living people, without mentioning a definite time, you often use ____________

Also see unit 36

# 14 The passive 1

**Look at the picture and answer the question using the verb given. The answer always begins *I'm afraid it ...* . Be careful: the tense in your answer should be the same as that in the question.**

Example:

What's happened to the train?
I'm afraid it's **been cancelled.** (cancel)

1

What's happened to your car?
I'm afraid it's ______________ (steal)

2

What's going to happen to the old town hall? I'm afraid it's ______________ ______________ (demolish)

3

What's happened to our house?
I'm afraid it ______________ (burgle)

4

What do you think will happen to the airport if the holiday trade increases?
I'm afraid it ______________ (enlarge)

5

What's happening to the traffic during the procession? I'm afraid it ______________ ______________ (divert)

6

What's happened to the sign?
I'm afraid it ______________
(knock down)

7

What happens to the waste paper?
I'm afraid it ______________
(throw away)

# Can you work it out?

**A Match the beginning of each sentence with the most appropriate ending, *a* or *b*.**

| | |
|---|---|
| 1 I gave | a) everybody my address. |
| 2 I was given | b) everybody's address. |

| | |
|---|---|
| 3 This tiger killed | a) by two hunters. |
| 4 This tiger was killed | b) two hunters. |

| | |
|---|---|
| 5 Pam has her own car because | a) she likes being driven. |
| 6 Pam has her own chauffeur because | b) she likes driving. |

| | |
|---|---|
| 7 Ian's a music teacher now; | a) he's being taught the piano. |
| 8 Ian's a music student now; | b) he's teaching the piano. |

| | |
|---|---|
| 9 At the reunion | a) he remembered all his old friends. |
| 10 At the funeral | b) he was remembered by all his old friends. |

**B Decide what speaker B says in each case, *a* or *b*. Notice that B speaks first in some of the conversations and second in others.**

1 **A:** Been working hard?
**B:** ____________________

2 **A:** Oh no! I've got paint on my shirt!
**B:** ____________________

a) Yes, that door's just been painted.
b) Yes, I've just painted that door.

---

3 **A:** Do you want to report something, madam?
**B:** ____________________

4 **A:** Are you chasing that man?
**B:** ____________________

a) Yes, my bag's been stolen.
b) Yes, he's stolen my bag.

---

5 **A:** He looks relieved.
**B:** ____________________

6 **A:** He looks tired.
**B:** ____________________

a) Yes, the roof's just been mended.
b) Yes, he's just mended the roof.

---

7 **B:** ____________________
**A:** It must have been the hill.

8 **B:** ____________________
**A:** It must have been the police.

a) My car's moved!
b) My car's been moved!

Also see units 31, 32

# 15 The past 1

**Complete the story using the verbs below each picture. You will need to use the past simple, the past continuous, the past perfect simple or the past perfect continuous. Sometimes the past perfect is obligatory and sometimes it is optional. When it is optional give both alternatives.**

be drive can

It ___was___ early morning. I 1 ______________ all night to get to Sheila before she 2 ______________ leave for South America.

arrive not be have

I 3 ______________ at the hotel at 6 a m. She 4 ______________ in her room so I 5 ______________ plenty of time to prepare.

come wait

When Sheila 6 ______________ in I 7 ______________ for her.

not look see tell

She 8 ______________ surprised when she 9 ______________ me. Someone 10 ______________ her to expect me.

give drink feel fall

She 11 ______________ me a drink. I 12 ______________ it. I 13 ______________ a pain in my stomach and 14 ______________ on the floor.

kill not be confess hide say

'Now you'll never tell anyone that I 15 ______________ Floosie Moore,' she 16 ______________ . But it 17 ______________ important; she 18 ______________ and I 19 ______________ microphones all over the room.

# Can you work it out?

**A Choose the correct ending for each of the following sentences, *a* or *b*.**

| | |
|---|---|
| 1 I pretended I was asleep | a) so I said 'What time is it?' and yawned. |
| 2 I pretended I'd been asleep | b) so I didn't move a muscle. |
| 3 John repaired it because he did it | a) all the time in his job. |
| 4 John repaired it because he'd done it | b) before. |
| 5 When the manager arrived, they were robbing the bank | a) so she wasn't able to see the robbers herself. |
| 6 When the manager arrived they had robbed the bank | b) so she was able to see the robbers herself. |
| 7 She said it was raining | a) so we would need an umbrella. |
| 8 She said it had been raining | b) but that now it was clear. |
| 9 The *past perfect* is used | a) for an action completed before other past actions began. |
| 10 The *past simple* or *continuous* is used | b) either for a single action or for actions that happened at about the same time. |

**B Decide which is the correct phrase to complete the sentence.**

1 They felt exhausted that morning because *they drove/they had been driving* all night.
2 The village *was deserted/had been deserted* for years when we first visited it.
3 She understood the company's problems because she *worked/had worked* there since it started.
4 He *died/had died* at the moment he hit the ground.

**C These pairs of sentences are identical except that the first sentence contains the past simple while the second contains the past perfect. Write *different* if the past perfect changes the meaning of the previous sentence and *same* if it does not.**

**Example:** I knew he didn't lie./I knew he hadn't lied. different
1 They only arrived after I left./They only arrived after I had left. ______
2 She visited a woman who worked for the CIA./She visited a woman who had worked for the CIA. ______
3 He asked me if I ever sold antiques./He asked me if I had ever sold antiques.
______
4 They wouldn't let us in until we showed them our identity cards./They wouldn't let us in until we had shown them our identity cards. ______

**D Match each beginning on the left with its correct ending on the right.**

| | |
|---|---|
| 1 The past perfect is not usually necessary to indicate a move backwards in time … | a) … in indirect speech and if there is no conjunction. |
| 2 The past perfect is usually necessary to show a move back in time … | b) … if conjunctions such as *after, before* and *until* already make the move clear. |

Also see unit 45

# 16 Conjunctions

**Your friend, Araceli, is going to visit London for the first time. Look at the questions she asks you about London. Use your thoughts with one of the expressions from the box to complete your answers to her questions.**

| unless | as long as | in case | although |
|---|---|---|---|

| Araceli's questions | Your thoughts | Your answers |
|---|---|---|
| **Example:** What do you think the weather will be like? | It's a good idea to take an umbrella as it might rain. | Bring an umbrella *in case it rains.* |
| 1 What's the best way to travel round the city? | The underground is fast and easy. It's only a problem if she wants to see the sights. | The underground is best ______ |
| 2 But isn't the underground very complicated? | You decide to give her a map because you think she might get lost. | Here's a map ______ |
| 3 What do you think about the Sunday markets? | You always enjoy them, but many people think they are too crowded. | Personally, I like them ______ |
| 4 And what about shopping in Oxford Street? | This is not a good idea, except if she wants to spend a lot of money. | I don't think it's a good idea ______ |
| 5 Do you think it's a good idea to see the Tower of London? | This is only a good idea if she can arrive early to avoid the crowds. | Yes, it's a good idea ______ |
| 6 What about that jazz club you mentioned? | It's possible to go. The problem is she will find it very noisy. | Yes, you could go, ______ |
| 7 Do you think I should try to get to Scotland? | This is a good idea, but only if she doesn't mind a long journey. | Sounds like a good idea ______ |
| 8 Is there anything else I should know? | It would be a good idea to bring extra money because she might want to buy a lot of presents. | Bring more money than you think you'll need ______ |

# *Getting it right 1*

**Jan has just married Gwyneth and has gone to live with her in Wales. Here is a letter he has written to his friend, Dan. He has made 23 mistakes in his letter. Write the letter in your exercise book and correct the mistakes. The number of mistakes in each paragraph is written at the bottom of the page.**

Dear Dan,

1 I'm writing to thank you for a wonderful present you gave us for our wedding. Today I'm at home because I lost my voice; in fact, I don't think I can speak again for the next two or three days. This gives me plenty of time to write letters!

2 We arrived to Cardiff just a week after the wedding. I like already Wales very much. Many people here want to know what are the differences between Wales and Denmark, but I don't think there are so a lot. One of the most impressive, perhaps, is the beautiful view of sea and mountains which I am seeing from our window. Of course, the language is also very different! Although my English has improved quite a lot I'm still afraid of make mistakes. As for Welsh, I don't think I'll never manage to understand it!

3 I haven't already found a job, but it's very important for me to find one soon as I can't settle in here unless I don't find one. I don't want to depend of Gwyn for ever! In fact, I had my first interview the other day. The interviewer was very interested to hear I was an import-export manager in a Danish company and all the reasons why I had left …

4 I also had a bad experience the other day. The roads here are such empty that I got into my car and completely forgot which way to drive! Eventually a policeman has stopped me and told me I had better be driving on the left. He warned me I could prosecute. He told me to report to the police station next week. Some of my friends say I have to pay a fine when I go.

5 By the way, what did happen to you after the wedding? I rang your hotel, but they told me you already left. Anyway, please let us know when can you visit. Gwyneth sends her love,

Yours,

Jan

6 P.S. I can't remember if you took any photos at the wedding so I'm enclosing a picture in this letter if you didn't.

| Paragraph | | | |
|---|---|---|---|
| | 1 – 3 mistakes | 3 – 4 mistakes | 5 – 3 mistakes |
| | 2 – 7 mistakes | 4 – 5 mistakes | 6 – 1 mistake |

Also see units 37, 51

# 18 Wish 1

**Read the picture story and complete John's thoughts below each picture. Use the verb in brackets in the correct tense.**

**Example:**

I wish I ___had listened___ (listen) to the weather forecast before I left.

1

Oh no. I wish I ________________ (check) the petrol.

2

If only I ________________ (have) some waterproofs.

3

I'd be able to get home if I ________________ (bring) a compass.

4

I hope they ________________ (see) me.

5

If they ________________ (not come) I might have died out here.

Also see unit 40

# Modal verbs 3

**Read the picture story in Unit 18 about John at sea. When the captain heard John's story, he was not very sympathetic. Complete the captain's sentences using the words in brackets with *should, would* or *could/might* (in this situation *could* and *might* mean the same thing) in the correct form.**

Don't your realise you ___could have drifted___ (drift) for days? You 1 __________ (even die) if we hadn't seen you. You 2 __________ (listen) to the weather forecast before you left and you 3 __________ (check) your petrol supply. You 4 __________ (not go) sailing again until you learn to do it properly. You were lucky we found you; we 5 __________ (easily miss) you out in the open sea and then you 6 __________ (be) in real trouble. If you went to classes you 7 __________ (know) what to do and you 8 __________ (learn) to be a real sailor, though I'm not sure of that. You 9 __________ (take) some waterproof clothes and a life jacket when you set out, and you 10 __________ (tell) someone where you were going. In fact, you 11 __________ (go out) at all as the weather's been so changeable recently. If you had died it 12 __________ (be) all your own fault, and you're not a child either; you 13 __________ (know) better. You 14 __________ (still catch) influenza, so keep warm.

Also see units 7, 11, 20, 29, 34

# 20 Modal verbs 4

**A Complete the sentences with a verb from the box. If two answers are possible, for example, *I would leave* or *I would have left*, give both.**

| finish | go | fall | (reach) | lend | find |
|---|---|---|---|---|---|

Example:

We get into port tomorrow; we should have reached port today but we lost time in the storm.

1

If I'd ordered the tickets earlier I could ________ on the China tour next summer, but I can't now.

2

I would ________ it to you this afternoon but, as you can see, it's broken.

3

Some scientists believe we might ________ a cure for cancer by the end of this decade.

4

I would ________ the report before the end of this week only my computer broke.

5

All the leaves should ________ by the beginning of December.

**B Harry is having some trouble with the builders. Complete the conversation using the verbs in brackets and one of these modals: *might, could, should* or *would*. If two answers are possible, give both.**

**Harry:** I thought you said the house would be finished (finish) before next year.

**Builder:** Yes, well, it 1 ________ (be) for sure but for the rain. We 2 ________ (finish) building the house by winter if we'd been able to dig the foundations earlier and we 3 ________ (dig) them last week if we wanted to keep to the plan.

**Harry:** But we do want to keep to the plan.

**Builder:** Yes, we 4 ________ (certainly/finish) the foundations earlier, but with all the flooding the house 5 ________ (fall) down too.

**Harry:** I see. So what's the new timetable?

**Builder:** If all goes well we 6 ________ (finish) the interior by spring, and if so, you 7 ________ (move) in before the summer.

# Can you work it out?

**A Match each sentence on the left with one on the right.**

1 Do you know what the next stop is?
2 Do you know what the last stop was?

a) It could/might/should have been Leeds.
b) It could/might/should be Leeds.

---

3 How many of these tablets do I take?
4 Those tablets made me feel sick.

a) You should only have taken one.
b) You should only take one.

---

5 Why not come to the party tomorrow?
6 Why didn't you come to the party yesterday?

a) I'm sure you would enjoy it.
b) I'm sure you would have enjoyed it.

---

7 He might/should/would stay
8 He might/should/would have stayed

a) always refers to the present/future.
b) often refers to the past.

**B Match the beginning of sentences on the left with the ending on the right.**

1 It's a shame Sarah's gone abroad;
2 Let's give Sarah a ring and ask her to come

a) I'm sure she'd enjoy this party.
b) I'm sure she'd have enjoyed this party.

---

3 If they haven't sold all the tickets yet
4 I wish they hadn't sold all the tickets;

a) I might/could leave tomorrow.
b) I might/could have left tomorrow.

---

5 She would/could/might stay
6 She would/could/might have stayed

a) refers to a future which is still possible.
b) often refers to a present/future which is no longer possible.

**C Put a tick ✓ against the endings which are possible. Sometimes both *a* and *b* are possible, sometimes only one of them is.**

1 Why not wait here until 7.00?
a) He might/could/should phone by then. ☐
b) He might/could/should have phoned by then. ☐

2 Why not get here at 7.00?
a) He might/could/should phone any time after then. ☐
b) He might/could/should have phoned any time after then. ☐

3 To get the diploma you
a) should attend 1000 hours by the end of the course. ☐
b) should have attended 1000 hours by the end of the course. ☐

4 We'll let him take the exam again at the end of the week;
a) he might/could understand calculus by then. ☐
b) he might/could have understood calculus by then. ☐

5 Paris is such a beautiful city;
a) everybody should go there at least once in their life. ☐
b) everybody should have been there at least once in their life. ☐

6 It might/could/should/would have happened
a) can refer to the past, present or future. ☐
b) can only refer to the present/future. ☐

7 It might/should/would happen
a) can refer to the past, present or future. ☐
b) can only refer to the present/future. ☐

Also see units 7, 11, 19, 29, 34

# 21 Substitution words

**Your friend, Mariana, has just arrived to stay with you in your flat. She asks you some questions. Complete your replies to her questions using the verb given, in the correct form, and one of the words from the box.**

| | | | | |
|---|---|---|---|---|
| so | myself | that | one | |
| them | not | this | any | it |
| (yourself) | some | to | | |

| Mariana's questions | Your replies |
|---|---|
| **Example:** Can I make some coffee? | No need to ask. Just help yourself! (help) |
| 1 Do you have any milk? | Sorry, I don't think I ________ (have got) |
| 2 Where's the nearest shop? | Don't worry about the shops. I'm sure my neighbour ________ (lend) |
| 3 By the way, do you feel like watching a video tonight? | I'm afraid I'm feeling rather tired so I don't really ________ (want) |
| 4 Well, how about watching it tomorrow instead? | Sounds fine; I ________ (prefer) |
| 5 Do you think you'll be late back from work tomorrow? | Well, I ________ (hope) |
| 6 And are you free on Friday evening? | I'll have to check, but I ________ (think) |
| 7 In that case, why not give Sam and Ella a ring? | OK. I'll try not to forget to ________ (phone) |
| 8 Do you still have their number? | No, I don't. I think I must ________ (lose) |
| 9 Do you need some paper to write it on? | That's OK, thanks. I can just ________ (use) |
| 10 I saw your book. Are you learning French? | Well, I haven't got very far, but I'm trying to ________ (teach) |
| 11 One last thing, could I read your newspaper? | Sorry, but I've been so busy that I ________ (not buy) |

# Can you work it out?

**A This is part of a conversation between two people. Decide which replies are possible. In each case, one is *not* possible.**

**Example:**

**A:** How did you enjoy the party?
**B:** a) I enjoyed it very much. ✓
b) I enjoyed very much. ✗
c) I enjoyed myself very much. ✓

1 **A:** Would you like to see a film tonight?
**B:** a) I think I'll be busy. ☐
b) I don't think. ☐
c) I don't think so. ☐

2 **A:** Oh, why's that?
**B:** a) I have to meet someone. ☐
b) I have to meet someone else. ☐
c) I have to meet another person. ☐

3 **A:** Could I see you for just a short time?
**B:** a) I'm afraid not; I won't have time. ☐
b) I'm afraid no; I won't have time. ☐
c) I'm afraid I won't have time. ☐

4 **A:** Would you like to watch TV tomorrow?
**B:** a) Yes, I would. ☐
b) Yes, I'd like. ☐
c) Yes, I'd like to. ☐

5 **A:** OK, see you tomorrow then.
**B:** a) Yes, I hope it. ☐
b) Yes, I hope so. ☐
c) Yes, I hope to. ☐

6 **A:** Shall I order you a pizza?
**B:** a) Yes, I'd like that. ☐
b) Yes, I'd like one. ☐
c) Yes, I'd like it. ☐

7 **A:** And what about beer?
**B:** a) Yes, get some. ☐
b) Yes, get them. ☐
c) Yes, get one. ☐

**B Use the pictures to finish what the people are saying. Include a word from the box.**

| some (so) one myself |
|---|

**Example:**

It should fit me; at least I *hope so.*

1

This is delicious rice. Why don't you ____________

2

I'm having a beer. Are you sure you won't ____________

3

This camera has a special timer so I can take photos ____________

# 22 The future 1

**A Doug has been offered a job with an international magazine. He has heard that the magazine has problems. Doug telephones the editor and makes these comments:**

Examples: 'I hear you produce only 1000 copies a week.'
'I hear you haven't moved to your new offices yet.'

1 'I've been told you sell to only four countries.'
2 'You don't have a computer network system.'
3 'Someone told me you don't have a marketing manager.'
4 'I hear salaries are very low.'
5 'I've heard you have problems with your printing press.'
6 'They tell me you only print in black and white.'

**The editor wants Doug to work for the magazine so he answers Doug's worries. Complete the editor's replies using a verb from the box each time.**

| sell | raise | solve | produce | install | print | move | appoint |
|---|---|---|---|---|---|---|---|

Examples: We *will be producing* at least 10 000 copies a week.
We *will have moved* to our new offices.

1 We ____________ to at least twelve countries.
2 We ____________ a computer network system.
3 We ____________ a new marketing manager.
4 We ____________ our salaries to a good level.
5 We ____________ our printing press problems.
6 We ____________ in full colour.

**B Use the signs to complete the phrases on the right with the verbs given.**

Example:

**BRIDGE CLOSED**
**FOR PAINTING**
**JUNE 10–12**

'It looks as if it'll be difficult to visit you on the 11th as I've noticed they (a) *will be painting* the bridge, but the 13th is fine as they (b) *will have completed* the work by then.'

paint
complete

1

**NO ENTRY**
**FINANCE MEETING**
**14.00-16.00**

'Can you tell me the decision at lunch-time?' 'Well, I don't think we (a) ____________ it by then. We (b) ____________ about it in the meeting today.'

take
talk

2

OFFICE HOURS
9.00–1.00 2.00–5.00

'Don't come in the morning because I (a) ____________ that report, but don't come after 5.00 either because I (b) ____________ by then.'

type
leave

# Can you work it out?

**A Denise is 25 years old. She is studying for a research degree in agriculture. She is due to complete her course next year. She has just been to her elder brother's 35th birthday party and this has made her think about the next ten years of her own life. Choose which sentence ending, *a* or *b*, is correct.**

| | |
|---|---|
| 1 In ten years I hope I'll | a) be passing my final university exams.<br>b) have passed my final university exams. |
| 2 In ten years I hope I'll | a) be earning a good salary.<br>b) have earned a good salary. |
| 3 In ten years I hope I'll | a) be having two children.<br>b) have had two children. |
| 4 In ten years I hope I'll | a) be writing my university thesis.<br>b) have written my university thesis. |
| 5 When Denise talks about an action *in progress* in ten years she uses | a) future continuous – *I'll be doing.*<br>b) future perfect – *I'll have done.* |
| 6 When Denise talks about an action which will be *completed* in ten years she uses | a) future continuous – *I'll be doing.*<br>b) future perfect – *I'll have done.* |

**B Here are some more of Denise's thoughts about the next ten years. Complete her thoughts and write each one in the correct box. Use the future continuous or the future perfect.**

| | | |
|---|---|---|
| live in a warmer climate | meet the 'right' person | work as an agriculturalist |
| pay back all the money my parents have lent me | publish the results of my research thesis | live in a comfortable house |

| Actions in progress in ten years | Actions completed in ten years |
|---|---|
| I hope I ______________________ | I hope I ______________________ |
| I hope I ______________________ | I hope I ______________________ |
| I hope I ______________________ | I hope I ______________________ |

**C Denise is talking about her research work in agriculture. Complete what she says using one of the verbs from the box.**

| face | contribute | double | find | feed |
|---|---|---|---|---|

By the year 2050, the Earth's population 1 ______________ so there will be twice as many people. That means we 2 ______________ twice as many people as today. I certainly hope that by then we 3 ______________ much better ways of producing crops in order to do this; if not, there is no doubt in my mind that the world 4 ______________ major problems. Of course, I hope my own research 5 ______________ to any solutions that have been found.

Also see unit 49

# 23 Used to

**Answer the questions explaining that there is or was a problem. Use the correct form of *used to* in every answer.**

| | | The problem | |
|---|---|---|---|
| Example: | 'How's your new bicycle?' | The new handlebars were strange at first. | 'It's great now that *I've got used to the new handlebars.*' |
| 1 | 'How's England? Are you enjoying it?' | You don't like driving on the left. | 'I will if I can ______ ______ |
| 2 | 'How's the new house?' | You have a tiny kitchen. | 'It's OK, but I ____ never ______ |
| 3 | 'Are you enjoying your stay in Sweden?' | You don't like the cold! | 'Yes, but I can't ______ ______ |
| 4 | 'You know London very well, don't you?' | You knew it well before it changed. | 'Not any more, but I ____ ______ |
| 5 | 'Do you like living in Cornwall?' | Sarah didn't like her new school at first. | 'It's very nice now that Sarah ______ |
| 6 | 'I hear you've gone back to university. How is it?' | You haven't studied for years. | 'I'm enjoying the life, but after all this time I ______ ______ |
| 7 | 'Do you think you'll enjoy your new job?' | You have never given people orders before. | 'I'm not sure; I ______ ______ |
| 8 | 'Do you play much sport?' | You played football before your accident. | 'Not now, but I ______ ______ |
| 9 | 'How's the new job going?' | You have never got up so early before. | 'I'm enjoying it, but I ____ still ______ |
| 10 | 'How are you?' | You have never been alone before. | 'Fine, but John's away at the moment and I ______ ______ |
| 11 | 'How's your new computer?' | The keyboard is different from usual. | 'It will be great when I ______ |
| 12 | 'You're very good at sailing.' | You did it a lot at college. | 'That's because I ______ ______ |

# Can you work it out?

**A Match the beginning of each sentence with its ending, *a* or *b*.**

1 I'm used to driving on the left — a) when I lived in England several years ago.
2 I used to drive on the left — b) because I've been in England for two years now.

---

3 I was used to cycling to work — a) because I did it every day.
4 I used to cycle to work — b) but I use the car all the time these days.

---

5 I used to go to bed late — a) and I can always get up early the next day.
6 I'm used to going to bed late — b) but I haven't got enough energy these days.

---

7 I was used to living in a small house — a) because I'd never lived in a big one.
8 I got used to living in a small house — b) when I was living in Japan.

---

9 I got used to the cold — a) after I'd been here for a few months.
10 I'm used to the cold — b) because I come from Siberia.

---

11 I used to have an open fire a long time ago — a) but I'll have to get used to it again living here.
12 I'm used to an open fire — b) because I've got used to it living here.

**B Match each expression on the left with its correct meaning on the right.**

1 *I used to do it* means — a) this is normal for me.
2 *I was used to it* means — b) this was normal for me.
3 *I am used to it* means — c) I did this regularly, but I don't any more.
4 *I'll get used to it* means — d) I wasn't used to it at first, but now I am.
5 *I've got used to it* means — e) I'm not used to it now, but I will be.

**C Match each sentence beginning on the left with its correct ending on the right.**

1 I used to — a) rice every day; I come from Taiwan.
2 I'm used to — b) eat rice every day but now I eat pasta mostly.
3 I got used to — c) eating rice every day when I go to live in China next year.
4 I'll get used to — d) eating rice every day when I lived in Japan last year.

**D Make as many combinations as possible using one item from each box each time. There is a maximum of five possible combinations.**

| | |
|---|---|
| used to + <br> be used to + <br> get used to + | infinitive (for example, *use* a computer) <br> verb -ing (for example, *using* a computer) <br> noun (for example, *computers*) |

1 ______________________

2 ______________________

3 ______________________

4 ______________________

5 ______________________

# 24 Relative clauses 1

**A You are explaining to a foreign friend how to get to your house. Complete the instructions using the words in the box.**

| |
|---|
| launderette pelican crossing chemist (traffic lights) playground newsagent shop assistant |

Come out of the station and turn left. You'll come to some lights that tell the cars to stop and go, which are called *traffic lights*. Turn right. Go past a 1 ________ (a shop that sells medicines), and a place where you get your clothes washed, a 2 ________. Take the next left. You pass a place where children play, called a 3 ________, and then you cross the road at the 4 ________, which says if it's safe to cross. Take the next right, past a shop that sells newspapers, called a 5 ________, and my house is the red one without a number. If you can't find it, ask the 6 ________, that's the person who works in the shop.

**B Put a tick ✓ in the box if the relative clause(s) can be used to end the sentences correctly and a cross ✗ if it is not possible.**

**Example:** A florist is someone
- a) that sells flowers. ✓
- b) who sells flowers. ✓
- c) sells flowers. ✗

1 A church is a place
- a) you pray in. ☐
- b) you pray. ☐
- c) where you pray. ☐

2 A rose garden is a garden
- a) where you grow roses. ☐
- b) you grow roses. ☐
- c) where roses grow. ☐

3 An orphan is someone
- a) who parents have died. ☐
- b) whose parents have died. ☐
- c) of whose parents have died. ☐

4 A washing machine is a machine
- a) who washes clothes. ☐
- b) which/that washes clothes. ☐
- c) you wash clothes in. ☐

5 A penguin is a kind of bird
- a) who can't fly. ☐
- b) which/that can't fly. ☐
- c) you can't fly. ☐

**C Finish these sentences with relative clauses using the words in brackets. Where a relative clause is possible with or without a relative pronoun (*who, that, which, whose*), give both alternatives.**

**Example:** A widow is someone (die)
a) *whose husband has died.*

1 Birthdays are times (celebrate)
a) ________
b) ________

2 Strangers are people (not know)
a) ________
b) ________

3 An alarm clock is a clock (wake up)
a) ________
b) ________

4 A vegetarian is someone (not eat)
a) ________

5 A playground is a place (play)
a) ________
b) ________

Also see units 39, 47

# Checking ahead 2



**Here are some of the structures dealt with in units 26 to 51. Match each sentence with the correct picture, *a* or *b*.**

a

**Example:**
I wish you would come swimming. — b
I wish you could come swimming. — a

b

a

1 This is the man he hit.

2 This is the man who hit him.

b

a

3 He tried cutting down the bridge.

4 He tried to cut down the bridge.

b

a

5 She has stopped talking to him.

6 She has stopped to talk to him.

b

a

7 When he rang she said she was using the computer.

8 When he rang she said she was going to use the computer.

b

Also see unit 1

# 26 Adverbs of time 2

**Decide which of the words in brackets completes each of the sentences. Put the correct word into the puzzle to discover the word hidden in the centre of the puzzle.**

1 I haven't __________ been here. (never/often)

2 __________ I arrived in Britain I haven't felt homesick. (since/while)

3 I think I've been there __________ . (never/twice)

4 We first met six years __________ . (now/ago)

5 I've __________ realised what you said. (just/ever)

6 I __________ used to come here and sit by the river. (yesterday/sometimes)

7 I promise to meet you __________ the end of the day. (before/during)

8 I __________ saw a play by Shakespeare. (ever/once)

9 By the age of twenty he had __________ finished university. (usually/already)

10 I'm afraid I'll be busy __________ six o'clock. (since/until)

11 I __________ see you these days. (weekly/rarely)

12 I'm sorry but I haven't had time to do it __________ . (now/yet)

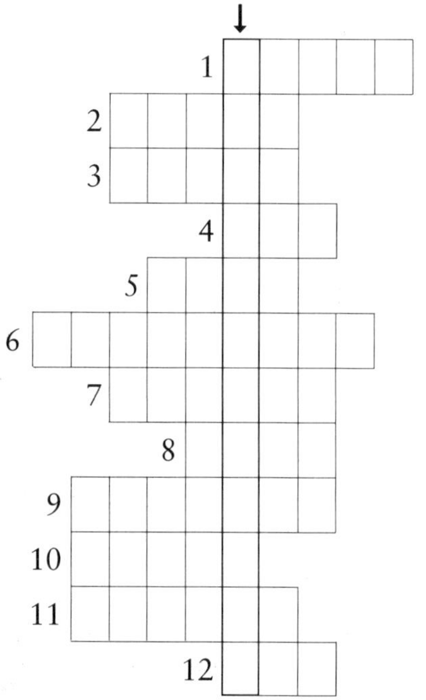


Also see units 4, 46

# Infinitive and gerund 1

**What are these people saying? Complete their sentences using a verb from the box in the correct form.**

| | | | | | | | |
|---|---|---|---|---|---|---|---|
| (listen) | watch | marry | feed | come | shout | tell | throw |

Example:

'Will you please be quiet; I'm trying *to listen* ________ to the music.'

1

A: 'What happened?'
B: 'I don't know; I remember ________ out of the door, then nothing else.'

2

'I don't regret ________ him; but I wish I hadn't said I liked modern art.'

3

'If I'm working at home I often stop ________ the sun go down.'

4

'Why don't we try ________ it against the wall?'

5

'I regret ________ you that the next boat won't be until May.'

6

'Will you please stop ________ and calm down.'

7

'I must remember ________ the cat.'

Also see units 28, 44

# 28 Infinitive and gerund 2

**A Complete the second sentence each time. Use the words in *italics* in the first sentence in the infinitive with *to*, for example, *to leave* or the gerund, for example, *leaving*.**

**Example:** I wish I hadn't *eaten* so much.
I regret __eating__ so much; I've got a stomach ache.

1 I couldn't *light* the fire because the wood was wet.
I tried ____________ the fire; but the wood was too wet.

2 I was cold so I *lit* the fire.
I was cold so I tried ____________ the fire, but I still couldn't get warm.

3 I *teach* every day. I never normally walk out of a lesson, but yesterday I felt sick.
I stopped ____________ and walked out of the class.

4 I was travelling through Arkansas when I was asked to stop and *teach* there for a while.
I was passing through Arkansas, but I stopped ____________ there for a while.

5 I didn't *lock* my car at first, but then I saw a poster saying 'Beware of car thieves'.
I only remembered ____________ my car when I saw a poster in the street.

6 I *went* to Greece as a child, but forgot all about it until saw the photographs.
I remembered ____________ to Greece as a child when I saw the photographs.

7 We *went* to the beach. When I saw how far it was, I wished I hadn't gone.
I regretted ____________ to the beach when I saw how far it was.

8 'I don't want to *tell* you this, but you must come with me to the station, sir.'
'I regret ____________ you that you must accompany me to the station, sir.'

**B Match the sentence halves on the left with the correct ending, *a* or *b*, on the right.**

| | |
|---|---|
| 1 He stopped eating | a) in a little restaurant outside Oxford. |
| 2 He stopped to eat | b) when he found an insect in his food. |
| 3 I tried to tell him a joke | a) but I couldn't remember it. |
| 4 I tried telling him a joke | b) but he still wouldn't laugh. |
| 5 He stopped to smoke a cigarette | a) but he still smokes cigars. |
| 6 He stopped smoking cigarettes | b) and then he went back to work. |
| 7 Did you remember to go | a) to Paris in 1979? |
| 8 Do you remember going | b) to the Post Office, or shall I go tomorrow? |
| 9 I tried to push the car | a) but I couldn't move it. |
| 10 I tried pushing the car | b) but the engine still wouldn't start. |
| 11 I regret to tell you | a) that you must leave this school forever. |
| 12 I regret telling you | b) my secret; you've told everyone. |

# Can you work it out?

**A Read what they did first and what they did second. Then decide which sentence they would say, *a* or *b*.**

| What they did first | What they did second | What they say |
|---|---|---|
| **Example:** He used to smoke a lot | but he stopped five years ago. | a) I stopped to smoke five years ago.<br>(b) I stopped smoking five years ago. |
| 1 He was working but he stopped | and smoked a cigarette. | a) I stopped to smoke a cigarette.<br>b) I stopped smoking a cigarette. |
| 2 She remembered their appointment | so she met him at the restaurant. | a) I remembered to meet Jim.<br>b) I remembered meeting Jim. |
| 3 He met Helen a long time ago | but he can still remember her. | a) I remember to meet Helen.<br>b) I remember meeting Helen. |
| 4 I told Peter and he told everyone | so now I regret it; everyone knows! | a) I regret to tell Peter my secret.<br>b) I regret telling Peter my secret. |
| 5 I don't want to tell you, but I must so | I'll tell you now, 'You must leave.' | a) I regret to tell you that you must leave.<br>b) I regret telling you that you must leave. |
| 6 I wanted to close the window, | and I tried, but I couldn't. | a) I tried to close the window.<br>b) I tried closing the window. |
| 7 The traffic was loud, | so I closed the window but I could still hear it. | a) I tried to close the window.<br>b) I tried closing the window. |

**B Write each word or phrase in the correct box.**

| | | Which action happened … FIRST | SECOND |
|---|---|---|---|
| **Example:** I remember seeing him. | (remember/see) | *saw* | *remembered* |
| 1 I remembered to see him. | | ______ | ______ |
| 2 I stopped seeing him. | (stop/see) | ______ | ______ |
| 3 I stopped to see him. | | ______ | ______ |
| 4 I regret telling you. | (regret/tell) | ______ | ______ |
| 5 I regret to tell you. | | ______ | ______ |

| I wanted to help him, so … | | She couldn't help him … |
|---|---|---|
| 6 … I tried talking to him. | (although she talked/ because she couldn't talk) | ______________ to him. |
| 7 … I tried to talk to him. | | ______________ to him. |

Also see units 27, 44

# 29 Modal verbs 5

**A Here are three photos. Decide which comment refers to which picture and write the letter of the comment in the box under the picture.**

i) **Example:** It must be cold.
   a) It might be cold.
   b) It can't be cold.

ii) c) People can't be working today.
   d) People must be working today.
   e) People might be working today.

iii) f) It might have been snowing.
   g) It can't have been snowing.
   h) It must have been snowing.

iv) i) The picture could have been taken in Britain.
   j) The picture couldn't have been taken in Britain.
   k) The picture must have been taken in Britain.

**B Here are some explanations of the comments above. Write the letter of each comment before the appropriate explanation. Note that the numbers, (i to iv), refer to the comments under the same number in part A.**

i) **Example:** Example because everyone is wearing thick coats.
   1 ________ because everyone is wearing summer clothes.
   2 ________ because the wind is blowing.

ii) 3 ________ because all the shops and offices are open.
   4 ________ because there is a lot of traffic in the street.
   5 ________ because all the shops and offices are closed.

iii) 6 ________ because the ground looks white.
   7 ________ because it looks quite cold.
   8 ________ because the sun is shining and the flowers are blooming.

iv) 9 ________ because people are driving on the right.
   10 ________ because the signs are written in English.
   11 ________ because there is a British flag flying.

# Can you work it out?

**A Read the information on the left and then use the verbs in the boxes to complete the comments.**

| might won't will could |
|---|

1 In winter, it's always cold in Mongolia. It's sometimes sunny and it sometimes snows. It's never foggy.

So when we get to Mongolia next winter it (a) ________ be sunny, it (b) ________ be foggy, but it (c) ________ be cold and it (d) ________ be snowing.

| could must can't might |
|---|

2 Colin is tall with a moustache. Paul is tall and has grey hair. Deb is short and has grey hair.

I can see someone coming: it's someone with grey hair, it (a) ________ be Deb, or it (b) ________ be Paul, but it certainly (c) ________ be Colin. Ah yes, I can see better now; it's a man and he's quite tall so it (d) ________ be Paul.

| must have might have could have can't have |
|---|

3 **A:** Have you ever seen 'Purple Turtles'? It's a great film!

**B:** No, I've never heard of it so I'm sure I (a) ____________ seen it.
**C:** Well, it sounds a bit familiar; I think I (b) ____________ seen it.
**D:** I'm not sure; I can never remember films, but I (c) ____________ seen it.
**C:** Oh yes, I remember it! I (d) ____________ seen it years ago!

**B Complete the sentences using the verbs in the box in the correct form.**

| will can could must might |
|---|

**Example:** When you are sure about something in the future you say it ___will___ or ___won't___ happen.

1 When you think it possible that something will happen in the future you say it ________ or ________ happen.
2 When you are sure that something is true you say it ________ be true.
3 When you are sure that something isn't true you say it ________ or ________ be true.
4 When you think it possible that something is true you say it ________ or ________ be true.
5 When you are sure that something has happened in the past you say it ________ happened.
6 When you are sure that something didn't happen in the past you say it ________ or ________ happened.
7 When you think it possible that something happened in the past you say it ________ or ________ happened.

Also see units 7, 11, 19, 20, 34

# 30 Countable and uncountable 2

**A The words in the box are the answers to clues 1 to 12. Nine of the words are nearly always uncountable and four are nearly always countable. Write the answers to the clues in the correct column.**

| |
|---|
| travel accommodation secrecy (research) sheep advice furniture people information teeth countryside work mice |

**Example:**

It's usually scientific.

1 They chew.
2 It's the opposite of *city*.
3 It includes tents, houses, flats and rooms.
4 Cats chase them.
5 It's the opposite of openness.
6 People love giving it but hate taking it.
7 They live in flocks.
8 It is supposed to broaden the mind.
9 Your home would be empty without it.
10 They are the most dangerous animals on earth.
11 It's at the heart of modern technology.
12 It brings in money.

| uncountable | countable |
|---|---|
| research | |

**B The words in the box are not really countable or uncountable, but six are always singular and six always plural. Put the words in the correct column.**

| |
|---|
| the news the police scissors each (of them) politics either (of them) the poor both (of them) everyone all (of them) trousers maths |

| always singular ( ______ is) | always plural ( ______ are) |
|---|---|
| | |

Also see units 2, 48

# The passive 2



**Decide which phrase, *a* or *b*, best completes each excerpt.**

Example:

**COLLEGE GUIDE**

The college was founded early in the eighteenth century, and some of the present buildings date from that time.

**a) The buildings which today form the the main quadrangle were added**
**b) They added the buildings which today form the main quadrangle**

early this century. The remaining out-buildings were completed between the wars when the college took on much of the appearance it has today.

1

**QUEEN VISITS BRIDLINGTON**

The Queen was dressed in a white suit with blue trim. She was wearing a white scarf and carried other white accessories.

**a) Her suit was specially designed for the occasion by Gocci.**
**b) Gocci specially designed her suit for the occasion.**

She was accompanied by her husband, the Duke, who also wore blue.

2

**CUTHBERTS RETIRE**

Sid and Joan Cuthbert have been running the Meadows Transport Cafe for the past twenty-five years. This has meant a regular routine of rising at 4.00 am each day in order to prepare around 350 breakfast eggs.

a) Some 600 slices of bread are also regularly buttered each day.
b) The Cuthberts also regularly butter some 600 slices of bread each day.

On receiving their retirement gift from local drivers, Joan commented, 'It's been a lot of work, but we've enjoyed every day of it'.

3

**LOCAL GIRL IN ROAD ACCIDENT**

We now have some details of the accident which took place earlier today. It seems eleven-year-old Amelia Hunt was on her way to school, just crossing Barton Road, when

**a) she was hit by a car**
**b) a car hit her.**

Luckily, Amelia was not badly injured and, after a hospital check, she is now at home recovering with her family.

4

**THE TELEPHONE: A MODERN CONVENIENCE**

The telephone is now very much a part of modern life.

a) Alexander Graham Bell first invented it and
b) First invented by Alexander Graham Bell,

there is now at least one telephone in most British households. In fact, recent statistics show ...

Also see units 14, 32

# 32 The passive 3

**Here are some excerpts from newspaper articles. There is a sentence, or part of a sentence, missing from each article. Use the pictures to decide what the missing words should be. Include the verb given. Be careful; you need to decide if the missing phrase should be active or passive!**

Example: **BANK ROBBERY**

Early yesterday morning robbers broke into Smith's bank. ___They stole $ 500 000___ (steal) and then drove away in a stolen vehicle.

1 **CENTENARIAN ADMITTED TO HOSPITAL**

In the early hours of this morning, Mrs Anna Kay of 21 Louth Drive was rushed into the Ace hospital. Relatives said she had earlier complained of difficulty in breathing. On admission ______________________________ (examine) and it was decided that an early operation was essential. It is hoped she can be home in time for her 101st birthday next week.

2 **LOCAL MAN MAKES PROFIT**

Primrose Cottage was yesterday sold for a figure well in excess of £200 000. The cottage was owned by Mr Sam Webb who bought it in 1985. Over the next few years ____________ ______________________________ (renovate) to its present condition. Said Sam Webb, 'It may be true that I'm making money, but then again, I did all the work myself'.

3 **CAR FACTORY TO CLOSE**

Residents of Malham were yesterday shocked at the news that their local car paint plant is to close. Cars are at present assembled in nearby Dewby and then brought to Malham where ____________________________________ (paint). A local spokesman said the news could well mean the loss of over 100 jobs.

# Can you work it out?

## NEW HELEN O'NEILL FILM SOON TO BE RELEASED

1 Fans will be pleased to hear Helen O'Neill has made a new film entitled *Dusty Moonlight*. 2 It is the story of a young girl who moves from Ireland to Spain. 3 They shot the film entirely on location in Ireland and Spain. 4 Luca Lopez directed it and Pablo Mendes produced it. 5 People say Ms O'Neill's costumes are outstanding. 6 Gocci specially designed her dresses. 7 They have already nominated the film for several awards. 8 It is due to open in Edinburgh this summer.

**A In the above press report some of the sentences seem out of place. This is because the main subjects of the report are Helen O'Neill and her new film and some sentences have been given a different subject:**

**Example:** 3 They shot the film entirely on location in Ireland and Spain.

**This sounds out of place because we do not know who 'they' are. It is more natural to relate other information to the main subject:**

**Example:** 3 The film was shot entirely on location in Ireland and Spain.

**Look at the sentences in the report again and write what you think the subject of each sentence should be. Some of them have already been done for you.**

| | | | |
|---|---|---|---|
| 1 | Helen O'Neill | 5 | ________ |
| 2 | It (the film) | 6 | ________ |
| 3 | The film | 7 | ________ |
| 4 | ________ | 8 | ________ |

**B Use the new subjects from part A to complete the re-writing of the press report. Look at those sentences which have already been completed first. Notice that you do not need to change all the sentences.**

1 Helen O'Neill has made a new film entitled Dusty Moonlight.
2 —
3 The film was shot entirely on location in Ireland and Spain.
4 ________
5 ________
6 ________
7 ________
8 ________

**C Here is a short passage about Marco Polo's introduction of pasta to Italy. Use the words in the box below to complete the passage. Note that you need to use some of the words more than once.**

| Marco Polo | it | he | discovery | Italy | China | pasta |
|---|---|---|---|---|---|---|

Many people are surprised to learn that 1 ________ was first introduced into 2 ________ by 3 ________ who discovered 4 ________ during his travels in 5 ________ . 6 ________ probably had little idea how significant his 7 ________ would turn out to be. After its introduction, 8 ________ was quickly adopted as a national dish throughout 9 ________ . Today, 10 ________ is produced commercially all over the country and 11 ________ even exports several varieties to 12 ________ !

Also see units 14, 31

# 33 Articles

**A Complete the conversation by putting the words in the box in the correct place. With each word, add *a* or *the* if necessary.**

| | | | | | |
|---|---|---|---|---|---|
| life | children | violent film | good film | film | film |
| films | violence | violence | violent films | quality | |

**John:** I saw ___*a good film*___ on TV last night.

**Jane:** Oh? What was it?

**John:** 'Blood or Money'.

**Jane:** Was it 1 ______________ ?

**John:** Well, it was quite violent, I suppose.

**Jane:** I don't like 2 ______________ .

**John:** 3 ______________ is a natural part of 4 ______________ ; you can't escape from it.

**Jane:** But that's no reason for enjoying it.

**John:** Well, it's not 5 ______________ I enjoy; it's 6 ______________ of 7 ______________ that's important.

**Jane:** So why does it need to be violent, then?

**John:** It doesn't need to be violent but if you're going to make 8 ______________ about something important and real, it will probably be violent too.

**Jane:** That's rubbish. And anyway, I don't think they should show 9 ______________ with violence on television; there might be 10 ______________ watching, and I don't think it's good for them.

**B Risto has written an essay about unemployment. Here is the first paragraph. There are ten mistakes with articles (there are no mistakes with singular or plural nouns). Find the mistakes and correct them.**

*The unemployment is one of a most important problems in a world today. It affects all countries: not only South America, Africa and Asia, but also the Europe and United States too. And it is not just the modern problem either; it has been with us for the centuries. The unemployment destroys the people's lives, it breaks up family and it makes society poor. The question is; what can we do about it?*

# Can you work it out?

**A Four sentences are true and two are false. Put ticks ✓ against the true ones.**

1 You can use *a* with plural nouns, for example, *Can you hear a dogs barking?* ☐
2 You can use *the* with plural nouns, for example, *Can you hear the dogs barking?* ☐
3 You can use no article with plural nouns, for example, *Can you hear dogs barking?* ☐
4 You can use *a* with uncountable nouns, for example, *A water is boiling.* ☐
5 You can use *the* with uncountable nouns, for example, *The water is boiling.* ☐
6 You can use no article with uncountable nouns, for example, *Water boils.* ☐

**B Look again at the example sentences in part A. Put the four correct examples into the correct paragraph.**

a) Sally is in the kitchen with her young daughter, Claire.

**Claire:** Can I make the tea, please, Mummy?
**Sally:** Yes, but do be careful. Put some water in the kettle, put some tea in the teapot, and when ____________________, pour it into the pot very carefully.

b) Sally and Claire are still talking.

**Claire:** I don't really understand my science classes at school.
**Sally:** Why not? What don't you understand?
**Claire:** Well, for example, ____________________ at 100°C, yes?
**Sally:** Yes.
**Claire:** Well, why?

c) It is night. Helen and Simon are lost in a forest. They are alone.

**Helen:** Where are we?
**Simon:** I don't know.
**Helen:** Wait, I thought I saw a light over there, and listen, ____________________

d) José and Carmen live on a farm near a forest. They have three dogs. It is night.

**Carmen:** José ____________________
**José:** Yes, there might be something out there. I'll go and have a look.

**C Match what you say with what you mean.**

| You say | You mean |
|---|---|
| 1 Can you hear dogs barking? | a) You expect your listener to know which dogs you are talking about. |
| 2 Can you hear the dogs barking? | b) You do not know which dogs; they are new to you. |
| 3 Water boils at 100°C. | a) You mean water in general. |
| 4 The water's boiling. | b) You mean some particular water. |
| 5 Society isn't fair. | a) You mean a particular society. |
| 6 The society is meeting tonight. | b) You mean human society as a whole. |
| 7 the | a) You expect your listener to know which particular one(s) you mean. |
| 8 – (no article) | b) You do not mean any particular one(s). |

Also see unit 48

# 34 Modal verbs 6

**Yesterday, Steven Johnson, aged 52, rescued a boat with two children in it. These pictures show you what happened.**

**Here is part of an interview between Steven and a reporter about the rescue. Use the verbs given to complete Steven's replies. Use one of the following in every answer:**

| | |
|---|---|
| managed, for example, *I managed to find* | could, for example, *I could find* |
| just the verb, for example, *I found* | couldn't, for example, *I couldn't find* |

| Reporter | Steven |
|---|---|
| Steven, could you tell us what happened? | Yes, I was walking along by the harbour when I ___saw___ (see) the boat about 400 metres away. |
| Did you know there were children in it? | Well, 1 ______________ (hear) crying, which I thought was coming from the boat. |
| Why didn't you tell the life guard? | I tried to, but I 2 ______________ (phone) because the telephone wasn't working. |
| So what did you do? | I 3 ______________ (decide) to swim out and get it myself. |
| Were you frightened? | I suppose I was, really, but when I was young I 4 ______________ (swim) six miles without much trouble, so I thought I'd try it again. |
| Was the sea rough? | Yes, very, and I nearly went under a couple of times, but finally I 5 ______________ (swim) to the boat and then I just 6 ______________ (climb) on board without any trouble. |
| What happened then? | There was an engine on board, but I 7 ______________ (start) it, so I 8 ______________ (find) some oars and 9 ______________ (begin) rowing. |
| Wasn't the boat very heavy? | Yes, it was, and I'm not young any more, but slowly I 10 ______________ (row) the boat back into harbour. |

# Can you work it out?

**A Match the sentences on the left with the explanations on the right according to whether the sentence describes a single past action, or a general ability to do something in the past.**

| | |
|---|---|
| 1 He could sing beautifully as a child. | a) a single action |
| 2 He was feeling sick but he managed to sing the song right to the end. | b) a general ability |

| | |
|---|---|
| 3 Apparently, she was able to walk before she was one year old. | a) a single action |
| 4 She had broken a leg, but she was still able to walk to a house for help. | b) a general ability |

| | |
|---|---|
| 5 The horse escaped last night and we couldn't catch it. | a) a single action |
| 6 I couldn't swim until I was about 20 years old. | b) a general ability |

| | |
|---|---|
| 7 I didn't stop her because I simply wasn't able to. | a) a single action |
| 8 I've never been able to dance. | b) a general ability |

**B Put the correct form of *managed to, could* and *was able to* in the correct box.**

| | **To describe single past actions we use:** | **To describe general past ability we use:** |
|---|---|---|
| | **1** | **2** |
| **Affirmative** | I ____________<br>I ____________ | I ____________<br>I ____________ |
| | **3** | **4** |
| **Negative** | I ____________<br>I ____________<br>I ____________ | I ____________<br>I ____________ |

**C Match each beginning on the left with its correct ending, *a* or *b*, on the right.**

| | |
|---|---|
| 1 You cannot use *managed to* | a) for a single past action. |
| 2 You cannot use *could* | b) for general past ability. |

| | |
|---|---|
| 3 You use *able to* | a) to show ability, with or without effort. |
| 4 You use *manage* | b) to show success through effort. |

Also see units 7, 11, 19, 20, 29

# 35 Reporting

**A Use one of the verbs from the box to complete the report about each picture.**

| |
|---|
| (ask) warn suggest invite order (insist) remind tell |

**Examples:**

She __asked__ the hairdresser __to cut her hair very short.__

He __insisted__ the tourists __should visit Yorkshire.__

1 She ______ the dog ______________________

2 The waiter ______ the customer ______________________

3 She ______ the boy ______________________

4 He ______ his girlfriend ______________________

5 He ______ his daughter ______________________

6 The manager ______ her secretary ______________________

# Can you work it out?

**A Humphrey is a manager at a publishing company. He needs to appoint a new assistant. Put each of the verbs from the box into its correct sentence.**

| advised agreed thought wanted asked insisted<br>said suggested told persuaded reminded |
|---|

1 Humphrey *advised* the company to appoint a new assistant.
__________
__________
__________
__________
__________

2 Humphrey __________ the company should appoint a new assistant.
__________
__________
__________
__________

**B Choose the correct verb each time**

1 Humphrey *suggested/advised* them to put an advert in the local paper.
2 Humphrey *said/told* the candidates should come for an interview.
3 Humphrey *persuaded/insisted* the company to offer a good salary.
4 Humphrey *wanted/thought* his new assistant should do some of his work.

**C Complete Humphrey's report on some of the interview questions he asked the candidates. Use a word or phrase from each box in each question.**

| | | |
|---|---|---|
| if<br>what | previous experience<br>they had<br>they had taken<br>their last job<br>university course<br>they had liked | previous experience<br>they had<br>they had taken<br>their last job<br>a university course<br>had been |

I asked them __________. I asked them __________.
I asked them __________. I asked them __________.
I asked them __________. I asked them __________.

**D Here is Humphrey's report. Correct any of his sentences which are incorrect.**

**Example:** I invited several candidates should come for an interview. *candidates to come*
1 I asked them to tell me why they wanted the job. __________
2 I asked them have your worked for a publishing company before. __________
3 I asked what had been their previous job. __________
4 I also wanted to know what will they do in the future. __________
5 I advised some candidates should come back when they had more experience.
__________
6 I said the best two to come back for a second interview. __________

# 36 Past and present

**A Complete each person's question using *you* and the verb given.**

1

When __________________ the change? (notice)

2

Why __________________ your dog? (shave)

3

How long __________________ ? (wait)

4

How many times __________________ this before? (do)

5

How fast __________________ at the time of the accident? (drive)

6

How many people __________________ every day? (meet)

**B Complete the story using the verbs given.**

It was while I 1 __________ (live) in New Mexico that I first 2 __________ (realise) that I 3 __________ (be) on this earth before. One day at dawn I 4 __________ (climb) over the Aztec ruins, when, in the sun's first light, I suddenly 5 __________ (see) pictures that 6 __________ (draw) by Aztec priests almost one thousand years before. Staring at me from the stone 7 __________ (be) a face I 8 __________ (recognise) as my own. It 9 __________ (be) then that the dreams 10 __________ (begin), which 11 __________ (haunt) me ever since, of the days when I 12 __________ (sacrifice) men's immortal souls to the sun.

Also see units 3, 9, 13

# Getting it right 2



**Jan has married Gwyneth and is living in Wales. This is his second letter to his friend, Dan. He has made 23 mistakes in his letter. Write the letter in your exercise book and correct the mistakes. The number of mistakes in each paragraph is written at the bottom of the page.**

Dear Dan

1 Thank you so much for writing back such quickly. I'm afraid I still haven't managed to find a job, but I hope to get it soon. Fortunately, the person lives next door to us is interested in learning Danish so I am able to earn a little money.

2 Because Gwyneth is out all day I sometimes feel a little lonely. I really wish she wouldn't need to work so much. When I feel lonely I often can't stop to think about about my friends and family in Denmark, and I just remember to eat my favourite Danish food and all the other things I used do at home. Occasionally, I wish I didn't come here because I'm sure if we had stayed there Gwyneth could find a job by now. But anyway, I'm enjoying here on the whole although I'm still not used to hear the language.

3 I really like countryside round here and yesterday, because I had plenty of spare time, I could go for a long walk through the hills. I was frightened of getting lost, but eventually I could get home without too many problems.

4 I spend most of my time thinking about finding a work. Denise, the woman who husband I'm teaching Danish, has given me some good advices. She has suggested me to put an advert in the local newspaper. I really wish I found a good job. The local school needs an economics teacher, but economics aren't really my field.

5 Yes, I'd love you to come and visit as soon as possible. I hope that by the time you get here I have found a job. I'd like to ring you but I don't have your number any more - I think perhaps I would have left it in Denmark but I'm not sure. Is it possible for you to phone me? If so, please ring in the evening because I'll probably look for a job during the day-time.

Yours

Jan

6 P.S. Please remember getting in touch as soon as you can. Gwyneth asked me to remember to send you her love too.

| Paragraph | | | |
|---|---|---|---|
| | 1 – 3 mistakes | 3 – 3 mistakes | 5 – 2 mistakes |
| | 2 – 8 mistakes | 4 – 6 mistakes | 6 – 1 mistake |

Also see units 17, 51

# 38 Look, look like, look as if

**Mrs Wallace has just moved into Lucas Street. Her new neighbours have different opinions of her. Look at the neighbours' thoughts and complete their answers. Use one of the three forms: *She looks/ sounds …; She looks/sounds like …; She looks/ sounds as if …***

Mrs Wallace

## A What does Mrs Wallace look like?

Mr Toms thinks …

Mrs Porrit thinks …

Mr Payne thinks …

**Example:**
She looks like
a princess.

1 ____________ beautiful.

2 ____________ she'll live forever.

3 ____________ mean.

4 ____________ she'd murder you.

5 ____________ an old witch.

6 ____________ my old mother.

7 ____________ lonely.

8 ____________ she's had a hard life.

## B What's she like to talk to?

**Example:**
She sounds
charming.

1 Her voice ____________
____________ a silver bell.

2 ____________ she grew up in a palace.

3 ____________ an old crow.

4 ____________ she's hiding something.

5 ____________ aggressive.

6 ____________ she wants someone to talk to.

7 ____________ a brave woman.

8 ____________ Polish.

# Can you work it out?

**A Each of these sentences describes one of the pictures. Write the name of each thing.**

a

b
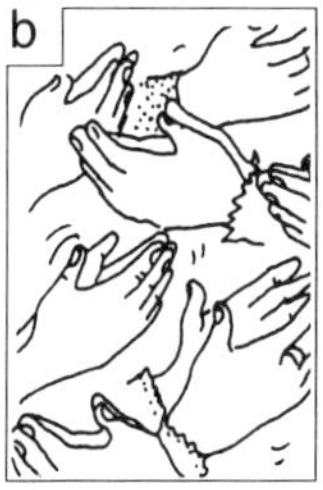
c
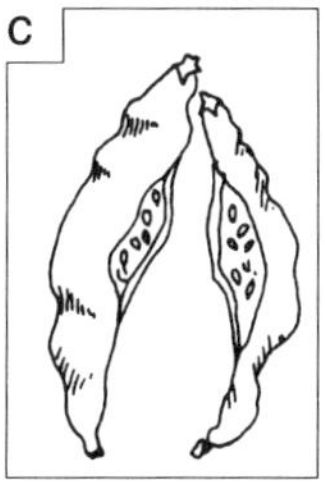
d

e

f
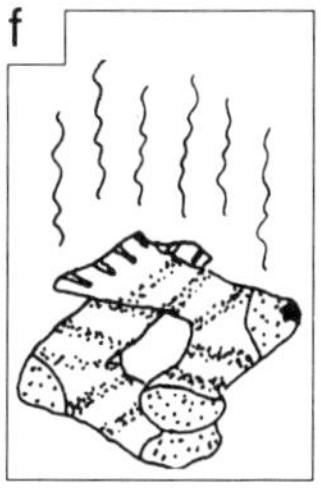

**Example:** It tastes like fire; it tastes as if it might burn your stomach away. c) chilli pepper

1 It feels hard and cold; it feels like a wet stone. ____________

2 They smell horrible! They smell as if they have been used to keep cheese in for twenty years. ____________

3 It sounds exciting. It sounds like waves on a beach. It sounds as though it could lift you and carry you away. ____________

4 He looks as if he has been running; he looks hot and sweaty. ____________

5 She looks old. She looks as though a breath of wind would blow her over. ____________

**B Put one of the following in each space <u>where necessary</u>: *like, as if* or *as though.***

1 Use ________ + adjective + noun, for example, *Monkeys look* ____________ *old men.*

2 Use ________ + noun, for example, *A cat sometimes sounds* ____________ *a baby crying.*

3 Use ________ + adjective, for example, *Cotton feels* ____________ *soft.*

4 Use ________ or ________ + clause, for example, *It smells* ____________ *something is burning.*

**C Look at the pictures and complete each sentence with words from the two boxes.**

| look taste smell sound feel |
|---|

| — like as if/as though |
|---|

**Example:** It feels rough.

1 It ____________ old fish.

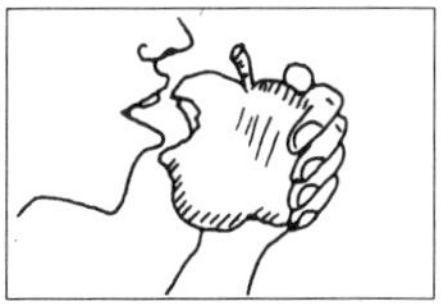

2 It ____________ sweet.

3 It ____________ African music.

4 It ____________ there's a party upstairs.

5 It ____________ it's going to rain.

# 39 Relative clauses 2

**Peter Wright had a strange experience last year and wrote it down. Now he wants to add some more information to it. Add the extra information using relative clauses with *which, who, where* and *when.***

> I was born and brought up there.

> 1 It's the first building in the village.

I went back to Fordham Green, where I was born and brought up, with an old friend called Melanie Dyson. We stopped at the church ________________________ because I wanted to walk down the road to the house ______________________________ .

> 2 I had spent my childhood there.

> 3 This is when my father died.

This was the first time I had been back since 1979 ______________________________ .

> 4 This wasn't surprising in the circumstances.

I was feeling very emotional ________________________ so I wasn't too surprised to see the figure of old Hilda Greenway sitting on a chair outside her old cottage. I stopped and said hello. She said hello, and then she just started telling me that my father didn't like the new motorway ______________________ and ______________________ . I didn't know anything about it of course, and I just didn't think about the fact that she was still alive although she must have been at least a hundred years old, if not more.

> 5 The council was building it past the village.

> 6 It was going to go through his favourite wood.

Well, anyway, just then Melanie ______________________ came up and asked me what I was doing. I turned towards her and said, 'Let me introduce you to Hilda,' and turned back again, but there was no one there. Hilda had disappeared.

> 7 She had parked the car and walked back.

I didn't know what to think. I described what had happened and what Hilda had said; and then how old she must have been ______________________ . Melanie ______________________________ didn't tell me I was mad; instead she took me to the doctor's house ______________________________ and I repeated everything I had seen and heard.

> 8 This is when I realised how crazy the whole thing was.

> 9 I trust her completely.

> 10 She had passed it on her way down.

Apparently Hilda had died twenty years before, at the age of eighty, but they really were building a motorway going past the village ______________________ so I believe I really did speak to the spirit of Hilda Greenway ______________________ .

> 11 It really would go through my father's favourite wood.

> 12 This is why I am opposing the plan to build it.

# Can you work it out?

**A Read the sentences and decide which statement, *a* or *b*, describes the defining relative clause and which describes the non-defining relative clause. Note that where there is a comma (,) in writing there is a pause in speech.**

| **Defining relative clauses** | **Non-defining relative clauses** |
|---|---|
| **Example:** Lambs *that are born early* are given special care. _a_ | Lambs, *which are young sheep*, are usually born in spring. _b_ |

| | |
|---|---|
| The relative clause tells you: | a) which particular group of lambs she is talking about.<br>b) more about lambs in general, ie what lambs are. |

1 Now I'm going to swallow the sword *that my assistant, Julia, is holding.* ______

2 Now I'm going to swallow the sword, *which my assistant, Julia, is holding.* ______

| | |
|---|---|
| The relative clause tells you: | a) more about the situation, ie where the sword is.<br>b) which sword he is talking about. |

3 Miners *who work underground all their lives* usually have health problems. ______

4 Miners, *who work underground*, usually have health problems. ______

| | |
|---|---|
| The relative clause tells you: | a) which group of miners have health problems.<br>b) more about miners in general; ie why they have health problems. |

5 The London *I knew 20 years ago* has gone forever. ______

6 London, *which I knew 20 years ago*, has changed forever. ______

| | |
|---|---|
| The relative clause tells you: | a) more about the situation, ie she used to know London.<br>b) which particular London she means, ie the one she knew 20 years ago. |

**B Complete these sentences by writing *defining* or *non-defining* in each space.**

1 You use a ______________ relative clause to tell your listener which one, or which particular group, you are talking about.
2 You use a ______________ relative clause to add extra information to your sentence; it does not usually help to identify which one/group you are talking about.
3 You do not use a comma in writing, or pause in speech, before a ______________ relative clause.
4 You do use a comma, or pause in speech, before a ______________ relative clause.
5 You can use *that* in a ______________ relative clause.
6 You cannot use *that* in a ______________ relative clause.
7 You can omit *who*, *which* and *that* if it is the object of a ______________ relative clause.
8 You cannot omit *who*, *which* or *that* in a ______________ relative clause.

Also see units 24, 47

# 40 Wish 2

**A Joachim, aged 4, is staying with his grandmother. He arrived about a week ago. In some ways she is finding his visit rather difficult. Look at some of the problems and then complete what she says using the verb in *italics*. Write each wish in the correct sentence.**

**Problems**

He *misses* his parents.
He doesn't *put* his toys away.
He *plays* with his food.
He doesn't *do* what I say.
When he arrived, he *said* he didn't want to stay!
He doesn't *like* vegetables.
He can't *dress* himself.
On Monday, he *hit* the dog!
Last week, he *broke* a very expensive vase.

1 Yes, we had several problems with Joachim last week:

Example: I wish he hadn't hit the dog.
I wish ______
I wish ______

2 Sometimes I think he really could behave much better if he tried; for example,

Example: I wish he would put his toys away.
I wish ______
I wish ______

3 But, of course, I know he's only a child so there are lots of things that won't change until he grows up, but still …

Example: I wish he liked vegetables.
I wish ______
I wish ______

**B Now look at his grandmother's thoughts and complete what she says to Joachim using the verb in *italics*.**

**Thoughts**

| | |
|---|---|
| Example: You *scratched* my car. | I wish you hadn't scratched my car. |
| 1 You don't *play* by yourself. | I wish ______ |
| 2 You've *lost* your favourite toy. | I wish ______ |
| 3 You can't *read*. | I wish ______ |
| 4 You *sing* at 6.00 every morning. | I wish ______ |
| 5 I *shouted* at you last week. | I wish ______ |
| 6 Yesterday, you *tore* my favourite book. | I wish ______ |
| 7 You *chase* the dog. | I wish ______ |
| 8 You *haven't* any other children to play with. | I wish ______ |
| 9 You *aren't* old enough to understand how difficult you are. | I wish ______ |

# Can you work it out?

**A Match the picture, *a* or *b*, with the wish.**

a

1 I wish you could speak to me.
2 I wish you would speak to me.

b

a

3 I wish you would buy me a walkman.
4 I wish you had bought me a walkman.

b

a

5 I wish you would get your hair cut.
6 I wish you had shorter hair.

b

**B Match each wish with the most appropriate ending, *a* or *b*.**

7 I wish it didn't rain so much in England
8 I wish it hadn't rained so much in England

a) then we could have seen much more.
b) then we could spend our holiday there.

---

9 I wish you would listen to me;
10 I wish you had listened to me;

a) I could help you so much.
b) I could have helped you so much.

**C Use the wishes in parts A and B to answer the questions.**

1 Which of the wishes can be re-written in the form 'Please … !'?

_2_ Please _speak to me_! ____ Please ____________!
____ Please ____________! ____ Please ____________!

2 Which of the wishes refer only to the past? _4_ ____ ____

3 Which of the wishes refer to a dream about changing something in the present? _1_ ____ ____

**D Match the description with the correct form.**

1 To talk about something in the past which you can't change now you use
2 To make a request for change in the future or to talk about possible future change you use
3 To express a dream about changing something which exists you use

a) wish + simple past *(I wish you did X)*
b) wish + past perfect *(I wish you had done X)*
c) wish + would *(I wish you would do X)*

Also see unit 18

# 41 Simple and continuous

In the year AD 79 in Italy, the volcano Vesuvius erupted. The lava and ash covered the town nearby, which is called Pompeii. It was very sudden and many people were killed where they stood. Here is one of the houses in Pompeii as it is now.

**Look at the pictures and complete the sentences in the past using the verbs in boxes.**

| stand keep (be) look |
|---|

This was the house of the Gaius family. It 1 ________ alone in what was a beautiful position. The walls were painted and 2 ________ very bright then. The Gaius family was rich and 3 ________ nine servants.

| be have weigh hold |
|---|

Marcus Gaius 4 ________ a swim when the volcano erupted. He was a fat man, and probably 5 ________ nearly 142 kg. The bath 6 ________ cleaned by two servants. It 7 ________ 355 000 litres of water.

| taste make weigh keep |
|---|

A servant 8 ________ a fish for the next day. The cook 9 ________ a fish sauce, a Pompeiian speciality. The sauce 10 ________ strong and salty; it was very popular. Another servant 11 ________ the family's dinner hot.

| stand have have hold look taste |
|---|

The Gaius family 12 ________ dinner. A servant 13 ________ a plate of meat for one of the family and another servant 14 ________ the food to check that it was all right for the family to eat. The master of the house, Julius, 15 ________ up at the time. He 16 ________ out of the window; perhaps he knew what was happening. We will never know what expression he 17 ________ on his face.

# Can you work it out?

**A Match each sentence with the correct picture, *a* or *b*.**

a

1 The machine shows you what he thinks.
2 The machine shows you what he's thinking.

b

a

3 'Do you have espresso coffee?'
4 'Are you having espresso coffee?'

b

a

5 'He's being funny.'
6 'He's funny.'

b

a

7 It's holding four people.
8 It holds four people.

b

**B Match the meanings on the left with the sentences on the right.**

| What you mean | What you say |
|---|---|
| 1 You want to know someone's opinion. | a) What are you thinking? |
| 2 You want to know why someone is quiet. | b) What do you think? |
| 3 You possess a shower. | a) I have (got) a shower. |
| 4 You are in the shower. | b) I'm having a shower. |
| 5 He is a funny person. | a) He's being funny. |
| 6 His actions at the moment are funny because he wants to make people laugh. | b) He's funny. |
| 7 It has four people in its hands. | a) It's holding four people. |
| 8 It is big enough for four people. | b) It holds four people. |

# 42 If sentences 1

**Complete the dialogues using the words in *italics* in the correct form. Be careful; sometimes the *if* sentence describes something different from what happened, for example, '*If we hadn't invented paper* we wouldn't have had newspapers; in fact we did invent paper.' Sometimes the *if* sentence describes something that possibly happened, for example, '*If the Chinese didn't invent paper*, then who did?'**

**Example:** **A:** Did Charles *get home late* last night?
**B:** I don't know. Why?
**A:** If he got home late ______ he'll be tired when he gets up.

1 **A:** Did the British *go to America*?
**B:** Yes, of course they did.
**A:** If they ______ the American language would be Spanish, wouldn't it?

2 **A:** Did Helen *catch the 10 o'clock bus* or the 11 o'clock?
**B:** I don't know. Why?
**A:** If she ______ she'll be here soon.

3 **A:** Did the prisoner *have a gun*?
**B:** No, he didn't. Why?
**A:** If he ______ he might have killed someone.

4 **A:** My new shirt's too small.
**B:** Did you *throw the receipt away*?
**A:** No, I've still got it. Why?
**B:** If you ______ you wouldn't have been able to take it back to the shop.

5 **A:** Richard took his exam yesterday.
**B:** Did he *study hard*?
**A:** I don't know. Why?
**B:** If he ______ he'll probably have failed; he's not very good at Maths.

6 **A:** Did you *tell* Peter you saw me in town yesterday?
**B:** No, I didn't.
**A:** Thank goodness! If you ______ him, I'd have been in real trouble.

7 **A:** Did the director *come in* yesterday?
**B:** No, she didn't. Why?
**A:** If she ______ she'd want to know why I didn't.

8 **A:** Do you know if someone *has invented* a speaking watch?
**B:** Yes, they have. Why?
**A:** Because if they ______ one, I would.

9 **A:** Has the rain *stopped* yet?
**B:** No. Why?
**A:** If it ______ we could go out for a walk.

# Can you work it out?

**A Put each of these *if* clauses into the correct box. You have to decide if they describe something which is/was possibly true, or something which is/was definitely not true.**

| possibly true | definitely not true |
|---|---|
| If the captain sent a radio signal | |
| | |
| | |
| | |
| | |

**Example:** If the captain sent a radio signal before the ship sank …
1 If the captain had sent a radio signal before the ship sank …
2 If Les had been here now …
3 If Les is here now …
4 If Sarah said anything to your boss while you were away …
5 If Sarah had said anything to your boss while you were away …
6 If Ali had bought the tickets when the box office first opened …
7 If Ali bought the tickets when the box office first opened …
8 If I have any more food …
9 If I'd had any more food …

**B Match each meaning on the left with the correct tense on the right.**

1 If you mean that it is possibly true in the present/future …
2 If you mean that it was possibly true in the past …
3 If you mean that it is definitely not true in the past/present (and even future) …

a) you use *if* + the simple past (for example, *If he left early yesterday* …)
b) you use *if* + the past perfect (for example, *If he had left early* …)
c) you use *if* + the simple present (for example, *If he leaves early* …)

**C Match each clause in part A with the correct ending below.**

**Example:** If the captain had sent a radio signal before the ship sank, ______ a) we would have been rescued by now.
1 ______ b) they'll rescue us soon.
2 ______ a) we'll be able to ask him.
3 ______ b) we could have asked him.
4 ______ a) you'll be in trouble.
5 ______ b) you would have been in trouble.
6 ______ a) we'll have excellent seats.
7 ______ b) we would have got much better seats.
8 ______ a) I'd give it to you.
9 ______ b) I'll give it to you.

Also see unit 50

# 43 Prepositions 2

**A You want to use the objects in the pictures but you don't know their names in English. How do you explain what you want each time? Use a preposition from the box to complete each of your descriptions.**

| with | through | on | in |
|---|---|---|---|

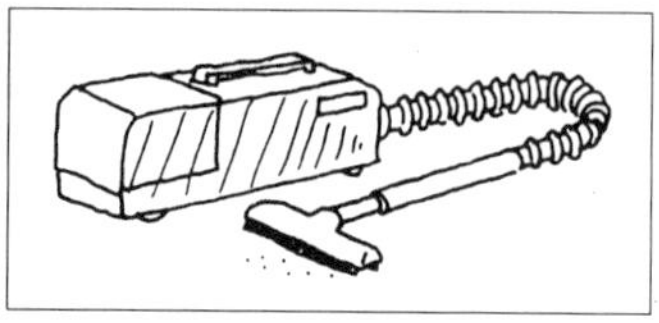

I need something to clean the carpet with.

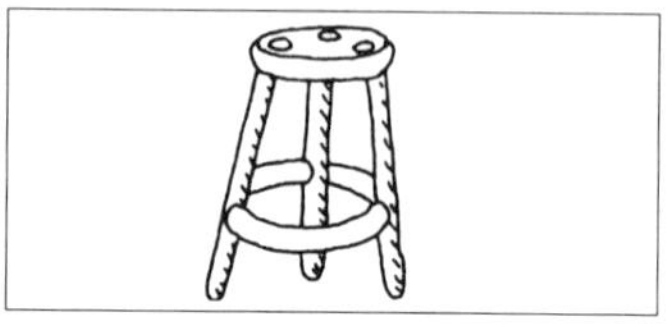

1 I want something to stand ______.

2 I need something to shout ______.

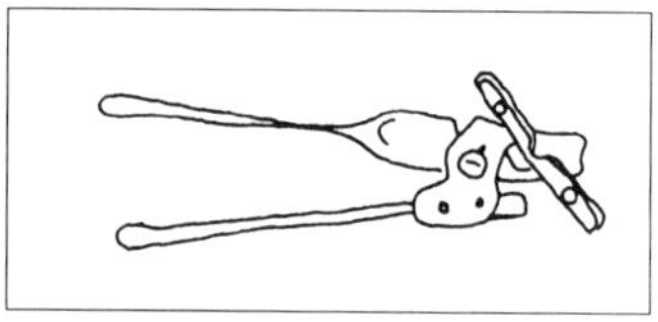

3 I need something to open a tin ______.

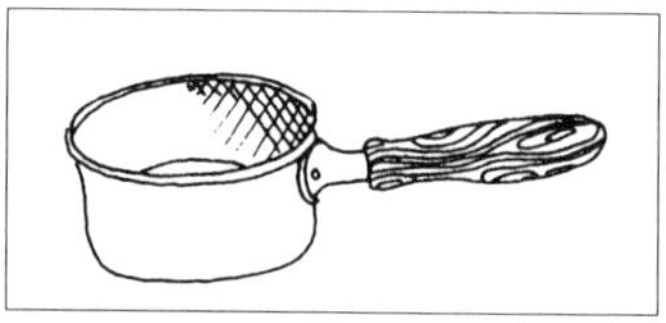

4 I need something to boil water ______.

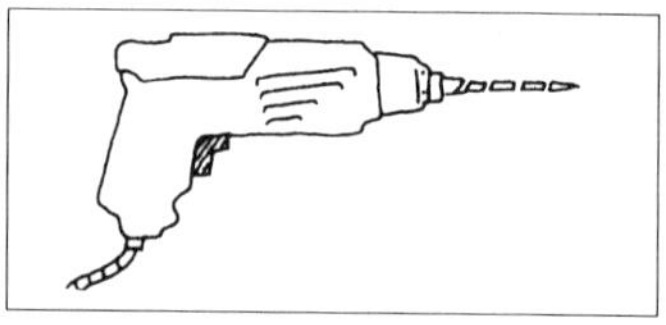

5 I need something to make holes ______.

**B Complete the answers to the questions. The pictures will help you. Include a preposition from the box.**

| in | from | on | with | through |
|---|---|---|---|---|

**Example:**
What's a credit card? It's a thing you pay with.

1 What's a straw? It's a thing ______ drink ______.

2 What's a dictionary? It's a book ______ find ______.

3 What's a safe? It's a thing ______ keep ______.

4 What's a library? It's a place ______ borrow ______.

5 What's a coat hook? It's a thing ______ hang ______.

6 What's a corkscrew? It's a thing ______ open ______.

Also see unit 5

# Infinitive and gerund 3



A There are 14 verbs in the box. Seven are followed by an infinitive, for example, *agree to do something*, and seven by a gerund, for example, *admit doing something*. Put the verbs on the correct side of the scales. The scales must balance and have exactly 40 letters on each side.

| | | | | | | |
|---|---|---|---|---|---|---|
| (agree) | avoid | choose | deny | miss | plan | recall |
| (admit) | arrange | consider | decide | manage | practise | refuse |

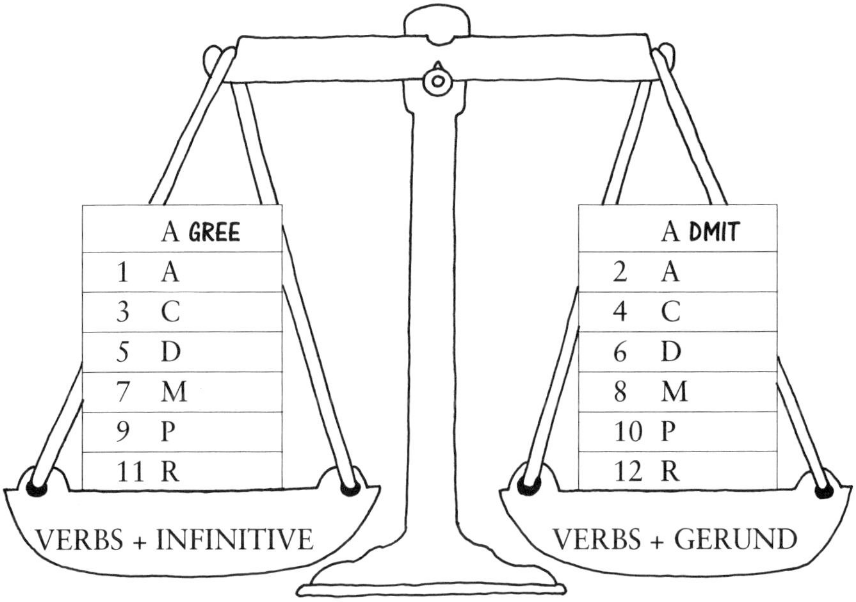


B Here are two conversations which use some of the verbs from the scales above. Complete each conversation by using a verb from the box. You must decide whether to use a gerund or an infinitive.

stay meet (see) get have

1 **A:** Sorry I missed *seeing* you last week. I was feeling so ill that I decided 1 ______ in bed; that's why I didn't manage 2 ______ to the meeting.
**B:** Well, never mind, we've arranged 3 ______ another meeting next week; we're planning 4 ______ at about two o'clock in the usual place.

attack give steal drop see

2 **A:** The accused doesn't admit 5 ______ the money, and he certainly denies 6 ______ the cashier. The cashier is refusing 7 ______ evidence because she can't recall ever 8 ______ the accused before.
**B:** In that case, I expect the police are considering 9 ______ the charges.

Also see units 27, 28

# 45 The past 2

**Frances is 80 years old. She is looking at some objects she has kept for many years and is telling a friend the story of why she never got married.**

> I was in love with and engaged to a soldier. His name was Tom, but he was killed during the war …

**Complete what Frances says about the objects using the verbs given.**

**Example:**

wear get married

Here's the dress I was going to wear when we got married.

1

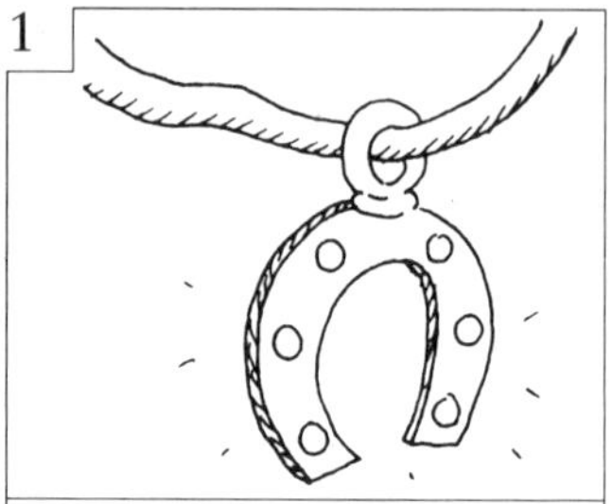

carry die

Here's the lucky charm he ______________ when he ______________ .

2

give promise

Here's the ring he ______ me when I ______________ to marry him.

3

see hear

Here are the unused tickets for a play we ______ ______________ the night I first ________ he was dead.

4

wear see

Here's the dress I ________ ______________ the first time I ______________ him.

5

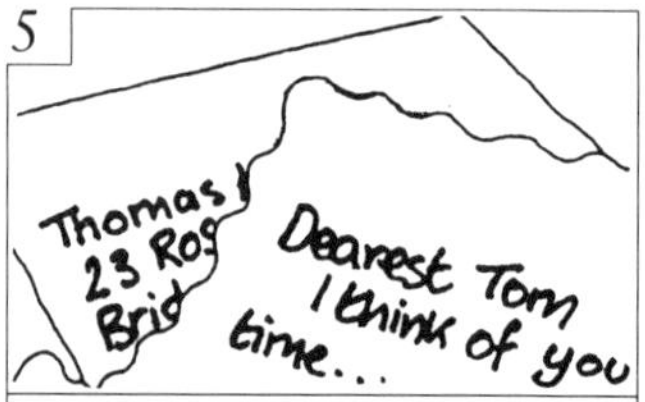


send die

Here's the letter, still unfinished, that I ________ ______________ him the night he ______________ .

6

tell write

Here's a poem he ________ me he ______________ specially for me.

7

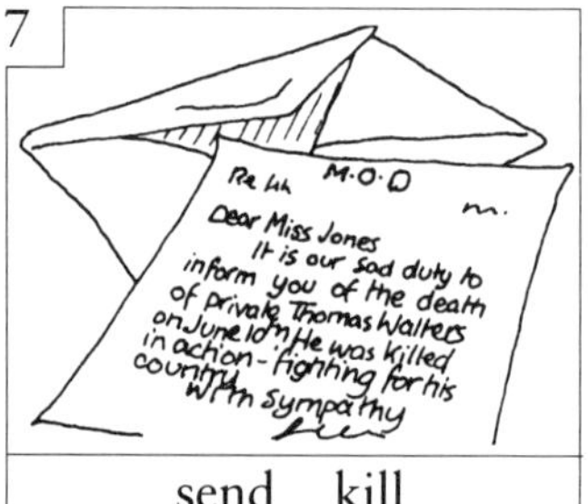


send kill

Here's the letter they ____ ________ to tell me that he ______________________ .

8

take meet

Here's the photo he ______ the first time I ____________ his family.

# Can you work it out?

**A Here are some photographs Sherry took on her holiday. They are of two friends, Alex and Karen. Complete what she says about each photograph using the verb given.**

**Example:**

When I took this one *Alex had (just) fallen into the river.* (fall)

1 When I took this one Alex and Karen ______________________ (climb)

2 When I took this one Karen ______________________ (get up)

3 When I took this one Alex and Karen ______________________ (eat)

4 When I took this one Alex ______________________ (have)

5 When I took this one the film ______________________ (finish)

**B Match the meaning of the verb with each picture with the explanations below and write the number of each picture in the correct place.**

a) an action completed before the photograph *Example* ________

b) an action already in progress at the time of the photograph ________ ________

c) an action only at the same time as the photograph ________

d) an action to start after the photograph ________

Also see unit 15

# 46 Adverbs of time 3

**A A tennis champion is talking about his friend, Ted. Fill in the missing words and then put them in the puzzle to discover who Ted is.**

1 Ted and I first met about three years ______.
2 That was ______ we both lived in London.
3 We've been working together ______ that time.
4 I've ______ worked so closely with anyone else.
5 We haven't ______ had an argument.
6 And we certainly haven't got tired of each other ______ .
**Example:** In fact we've _already_ had quite a lot of success.
7 I hope we can continue our partnership ______ many years to come.
8 ______ we go on working together I know things will go well.
9 I'm sure I ______ have a lot to learn from Fred.

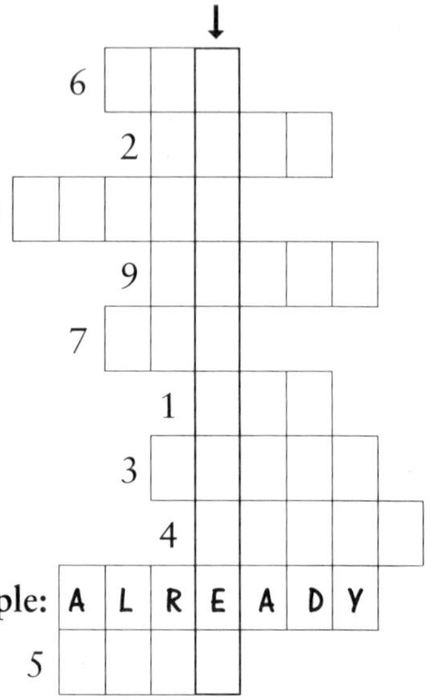


**B Philip and Jenny meet in Oxford. They haven't seen each other for a long time. Complete their conversation using the phrases in the box.**

| | | | | | | |
|---|---|---|---|---|---|---|
| (nowadays) | sooner or later | ago | whenever | over | these days | |
| present | ages | during | moment | long | time | every now and then |

**Philip:** Where are you living _nowadays_, Jenny?
**Jenny:** Well, I've been in Oxford 1 ______ the last six months.
**Philip:** Really? So when did you leave London?
**Jenny:** London? Oh, I left about five years 2 ______ .
**Philip:** And how 3 ______ do you think you'll stay in Oxford?
**Jenny:** Well, I'm quite happy at the 4 ______, but I suppose 5 ______ I'll want to go back to London again.
**Philip:** Are you still in touch with Paul and Sharon?
**Jenny:** Yes, I see Paul 6 ______ ; in fact 7 ______ he comes to Oxford but I haven't heard from Sharon for 8 ______ .
**Philip:** So who are you working for 9 ______ ?
**Jenny:** Well, I've been unemployed for a 10 ______ ; in fact I'm looking for a job at 11 ______ .
**Philip:** I'm sorry to hear that. Why don't you come over for a weekend soon?
**Jenny:** Yes, I'd love to; in fact it looks as if I'll have plenty of free time 12 ______ the autumn.

Also see units 4, 26

# Relative clauses 3



**A Complete the sentence on the left with the correct relative clause, *a* or *b*.**

| | |
|---|---|
| 1 King James I's Bible ___ is still a best-seller in its revised version. | a) , which was produced in English in 1611, |
| 2 He wrote most of his books in Latin, and the only one ___ was *The Temple.* | b) that was produced in English before 1611 |
| 3 The assistant ___ was Jane Carr! | a) you served |
| 4 The customer ___ was Chris Greaves! | b) who served you |
| 5 The detective ___ has just been suspended from the police. | a) , whom we arrested 5 years ago, |
| 6 The burglar, Joe Truman ___ has just escaped from prison again. | b) who arrested us 5 years ago |
| 7 That's not the thing ___ | a) , which annoyed her. |
| 8 He didn't understand what she said ___ | b) that annoyed her. |
| 9 That's Madha Jones ___ on the wall. | a) , whose painting, *The Party,* |
| 10 That's Madha Jones ___ is on the wall. | b) , who's painting *The Party* |
| 11 I'd like to introduce you to a person ___ | a) , who I've known since birth. |
| 12 I'd like to introduce you to Mary ___ | b) I've known since birth. |

**B Use the words in the pictures to write a relative clause in each sentence.**

Example:

That's Admiral Nelson, ***who fought at the Battle of Trafalgar.***

1

There were three apples ______________________

2

That's the woman ______________________

3

Whales ______________________ seem to have a complex language.

Also see units 24, 39

# 48 Articles and countable and uncountable nouns

There is one mistake or more in all of these signs and sayings. Correct the mistakes.

Example:

1 **If you need a help, please ask for an assistance**

2 All you need is the love

3

4 **Please leave a camera at the desk**

5

**Road jobs ahead**

6 Will all personnel please report to a main office.

7 **Advices Centre**

8 Collect your luggages here

9 **Now showing:**
*Travel to a centre of an Earth*

10

If you have the complaint, please ask to see the manager.

Also see units 2, 30, 33

11 *The beauty is in an eye of a beholder*

12 **Please turn off a light.**

13 **A sun rises in an east and sets in a west**

14 JOURNEY AGENT

15 Take the card; any card

16 Please ring a bell for a service

17

18 THE ENGLISH SPOKEN HERE.

20 **A foreign money not accepted**

19 *There is the time and the place for all the things*

21

# 49 The future 2

**You are in Britain travelling by train. Another passenger begins a conversation with you. Read the passenger's comments to you and then your thoughts about each comment. Use these thoughts and the verb on the right of the page to complete your replies to the passenger. You also need to use the most appropriate of the forms from the box.**

| |
|---|
| I'm ... ing<br>I'm going to ...<br>I'll ...<br>I'll be ... ing<br>Shall I ...? |

| The passenger's comments | Your thoughts | Your replies |
|---|---|---|
| **Example:** How far are you going? | You have a ticket to Cambridge. | *I'm getting off in Cambridge.* (get off) |
| 1 Why Cambridge? | You have arranged to meet an old friend there. | Actually, ______ ______ (meet) |
| 2 That's nice. Do you expect to stay long? | You have a ticket to leave on Sunday. | Not long, ______ ______ (leave) |
| 3 Any ideas what to do there? | You have decided to visit the colleges. | Yes, ______ ______ (visit) |
| 4 You really must see King's College Chapel. | You think this is a good idea, and you decide to go there too. | In that case, ______ ______ (go) |
| 5 Hey, I could take you there if you're free at about three on Friday. | You have plans to work in the university library all Friday afternoon. | I'm afraid ______ ______ (work) |
| 6 What a pity! Well, here's my phone number. Give me a ring if you like. | You wonder if 6.00 pm on Thursday is a good time to ring. | Let's see. ______ ______ (ring) |
| 7 Did you know you can buy coffee on the train? | You didn't know so you decide to buy one. | In that case, I think ______ (buy) |
| 8 Yes, it's quite good. | You want to offer the passenger a coffee too. | If it's good, ______ ______ (get) |
| 9 Oh, no thanks. I have to get off soon. | You want to remind the passenger about your phone call on Thursday. | OK. I ______ ______ (ring) |

Also see unit 22

# If sentences 2



**You have just arrived to stay with a British friend at her house. Read the comments your friend makes to you and your thoughts about the comments. Then complete your replies using the word *if* in each reply and the two verbs in *italics* in the 'What you think' section.**

| What your friend says | What you think | What you say |
|---|---|---|
| **Example:** Why don't you stay longer? You'd be very welcome. | You would like to *stay*, but you don't have time. | If I had time I'd stay longer. |
| 1 Why didn't you ring me from the airport? | You didn't *have* any change so you didn't *ring*. | If I ______ |
| 2 Do make yourself at home here, won't you? | You are happy to *help* yourself to anything you *need*. | Don't worry. If I ______ |
| 3 You know, you really shouldn't have brought all these gifts! | You *wanted* to *bring* them. | I wouldn't ______ |
| 4 Why don't you come and meet some of my friends on Thursday? | You'd like to *come*, but you aren't sure if you *have* time. | I'll certainly ______ |
| 5 Now, can you remember all the things I've told you about Glasgow? | You aren't sure if you *remember*, but you can always *ring* her to ask. | Don't worry. ______ |
| 6 And why not visit Cornwall too while you're here? | You don't *have* enough money! But you would like to *go* there. | Well, I think I would ______ |
| 7 Is Stephanie meeting us next weekend? | You know she was hoping to *come*, but you don't know if she *got* a plane ticket. | I'm not sure. She'll ______ |
| 8 By the way, it was a good thing you managed to catch the bus this evening, wasn't it? | You are happy you *caught* it because you didn't want to *wait* until tomorrow morning for the next bus! | Yes, I'd still ______ |
| 9 You look tired! Why don't you have an early night? | You are *waiting* for a phone call so you can't *go* to bed. | I would ______ |

Also see unit 42

# 51 *Getting it right 3*

Here are some common signs and notices. Complete each sign by choosing the correct word or words.

Example: If you *didn't use/aren't used* to strenuous exercise consult your doctor first.

1 These leaflets are free. Please take it/one.

2 **The police *is/are* to be informed if the alarm sounds.**

3 **Your life-jacket is under *the/a* seat.**

4 DENTAL CARE: Please remember *telling/to tell* your dentist if you are taking any form of medicine.

5 This medicine should/had better be taken three times daily.

6 We always try *answering/to answer* your call as soon as possible.

7 Bake for 45 minutes or until the top looks *like brown/brown.*

8 All visitors *should/could* report to reception.

9 If you wish you *would be/were* in the sun right now, give us a ring on 086 5416311 for the winter holiday of a lifetime!

10 *Who did do it?/Who did it?* Murder in Madrid – a detective thriller.

11 When you complete our course you can/will be able to take perfect photos.

12 No classes *will be taught/will teach* over the New Year holiday.

13 If you can't read this sign it can be/could be time for you to see your optician.

Also see units 17, 37

# Answer key

**Unit 1 Checking ahead 1**
1 b 2 a (see unit 3) 5 b 6 a (see unit 12)
3 b 4 a (see unit 6) 7 a 8 b (see units 19, 20)

**Unit 2 Countable and uncountable 1**

| | | |
|---|---|---|
| 1 time | 6 lights | 11 hopes |
| 2 times | 7 a light | 12 lambs |
| 3 glass | 8 light | 13 a lamb |
| 4 a glass | 9 hope | 14 lamb |
| 5 glasses | 10 a hope | |

**Countable and uncountable: Can you work it out?**
A
1 a 2 b 3 b 4 a 5 a 6 b

B
1 c) i) hairs 2 a) iv) a hair 3 d) ii) hair

**Unit 3 Subject and object questions**
A
1 directed 5 has
2 produced 6 does 'Time Out'
3 was it 7 does it/the film open
4 wrote

B
1 What poisoned Lord Mayhew?
2 Who did the butler see?
3 Who solved the crime?
4 Who wrote the novel?

**Subject and object questions: Can you work it out?**
A
1 a 2 b 3 b 4 a

B
1 a 2 b 3 a 4 b 5 b 6 a
7 b 8 a

C
1 Who wrote Hamlet?
2 Who landed on the moon in 1969?
3 How fast does light travel?
4 Who invented the phone?
5 Which countries border the USA?
6 Who designed St Paul's Cathedral?
7 What causes the sea level to change?
8 What did Neil Armstrong say?

**Unit 4 Adverbs of time 1**
1 I haven't read it yet.
2 I still haven't rung her.
3 had it since I went to India.
4 've ever met him.
5 already read it.
6 've never been to an Indian restaurant.
7 've had it for six months.
8 ever thought of employing a gardener?

**Adverbs of time 1: Can you work it out?**
A
1 I have already been to Australia.
2 I haven't been to Australia yet.
3 Have you ever been to Australia?
4 I've never been to Australia.
5 I still haven't been to Australia.
6 Australia is the most beautiful country I've ever seen.

B
1 c 2 f 3 d 4 e 5 g 6 a

C
1 It's the most beautiful picture I've ever seen.
2 I haven't ever been to Germany but I'd like to go one day.
3 You were talking about going to Munich; have you been there yet?
4 I'm trying to find someone who knows about Canada; have you ever been there?
5 Although Mongolia has opened its borders it's still difficult to fly there.

**Unit 5 Prepositions 1**
A

| | | | |
|---|---|---|---|
| 1 for | 4 to | 7 in | 10 of |
| 2 to | 5 in | 8 at | |
| 3 of | 6 in | 9 from | |

Hidden word: information

B
1 I can depend on
2 remember people by name
3 never criticise you behind your back
4 disagree with me sometimes, but not always
5 take advantage of other people
6 need to have a reason for everything
7 frequently get out of control
8 can't take pleasure in simple things
9 laugh at other people's misfortunes

**Unit 6 Enough and plenty**
1 just the right amount
2 there aren't quite enough
3 there isn't enough
4 there are plenty
5 there aren't enough
6 just the right number
7 there isn't enough
8 this isn't big enough
9 these aren't big enough
10 there is plenty
11 there are far too many

**Unit 7 Modal verbs 1**
1 Could/Would 5 should/could
2 could/might 6 could
3 could 7 could/might
4 would 8 would

**Modal verbs 1: Can you work it out?**

A

| | | | | | |
|---|---|---|---|---|---|
| 1 a | 2 b | 3 b | 4 a | 5 b | 6 a |
| 7 a | 8 b | 9 b | 10 a | | |

B

| | | | | | |
|---|---|---|---|---|---|
| a 7 | b 8 | c 3 | d 4 | e 10 | f 5 |
| g 6 | h 9 | | | | |

C

| | |
|---|---|
| 1 should | 5 could |
| 2 could, might | 6 would |
| 3 should | 7 would |
| 4 could | 8 could, might |

**Unit 8 So and such**

A

1 such 2 so 3 such 4 so 5 so

B

| | |
|---|---|
| 1 so warm/hot | 5 such a big/large family |
| 2 such a big/large house | 6 so long |
| 3 such a lot/so much | 7 such good food |
| 4 drive so badly | 8 are so many |

C

1 It was such a dark night that I couldn't see the path in front of me.
2 Then I saw a crowd of people, there were so many that I couldn't count them.
3 They were all glowing with such a bright light that it lit the path ahead.
4 I was going so fast that I couldn't stop.
5 But suddenly they vanished/But they suddenly vanished; I have never been so scared in my life before.

**So and such: Can you work it out?**

A

Noun phrases

| | |
|---|---|
| 4 such a lot of people | 8 such a little boy |
| 5 such delicious fruit | 9 such interesting people |

Adjectives and adverbs

| | | |
|---|---|---|
| 1 so kind | 3 so good | 7 so much |
| 2 so cold | 6 so fast | 9 so few |

B

1 ✗ so interesting
2 ✗ such a beautiful country
3 ✓
4 ✗ such a nice man
5 ✗ such nice food

**Unit 9 Indirect questions**

A

1 a family day excursion ticket to London is/costs?
2 if you have a double room available this weekend./if a double room is available this weekend.
3 it costs to hire a car for two days.
4 flight BA 272 arrives?
5 if you are open on Sunday evenings?/if the restaurant is open on Sunday evenings?
6 you can come and meet the Dumals on Sunday?/you would like to come and meet them on Sunday?

B

| | |
|---|---|
| 1 what time, ? | 3 if, ? |
| 2 whether, ? | 4 how long, . |

**Indirect questions: Can you work it out?**

A

1 e), c), a) 2 d), b)

B

1 ✓ 2 ✗ 3 ✓

C

1 Do you happen to know what time the next bus is due?
2 no change
3 Oh, do you happen to know where Comsoft Computer shop is?

**Unit 10 Advice**

A

1 Why don't you rent a car?
2 I think you'd better rent a car.
3 How about visiting Wales?
4 If I were you I'd rent a car.
5 You could always rent a car.
6 Have you thought of staying in a bed and breakfast?
7 Why not rent a car?
8 Perhaps you ought to come and stay with me.

B

1 of using a bicycle?
2 buy a CD player?
3 to have an eye test/to have your eyes tested.
4 look (them up) in a dictionary.

**Advice: Can you work it out?**

A

1 a 2 b 3 b 4 a 5 b 6 b

B

| | | | |
|---|---|---|---|
| a) | 2 b | 6 b | |
| b) | 3 b | 4 a | 5 b |
| c) | 3 b | 5 b | |
| d) | 2 b | 4 a | |

**Unit 11 Modal verbs 2**

A

1 Will you have to find a job there?
2 Will you have to learn Spanish while you're there?
3 Will you be able to go camping in the countryside?
4 Will I/we be able to write to you?
5 Will you be able to drive a car there?
6 Will you have to have lots of injections?
7 Will you be able to come home if you really want to?

B

1 do you have to be/must you be
2 can vote/will be able to vote
3 will have to start
4 won't be able to go
5 won't have to pay
6 must keep/have to keep
7 can do/will be able to do
8 will have to see

**Modal verbs 2: Can you work it out?**

A

| | | |
|---|---|---|
| 1 a ✗ b ✓ | 4 a ✗ b ✓ | 7 a ✗ b ✓ |
| 2 a ✗ b ✓ | 5 a ✓ b ✓ | |
| 3 a ✓ b ✓ | 6 a ✓ b ✓ | |

B

1 b 2 a 3 c 4 d

**Unit 12 Sense and actions**
1 Don't worry; I'm/I was only tasting it.
2 I don't know, but I can taste honey and nuts,
3 It smells of perfume.
4 I'm smelling this wonderful sea air.
5 I heard/I could hear voices but they've stopped now.
6 Please be quiet, I'm listening to the music.
7 Yes, in fact I'm seeing her tomorrow.
8 Yes, in fact I can see her coming now; look.
9 I was looking at that church; it's really beautiful.
10 I feel really cold.
11 I'm feeling the temperature.
12 I didn't/don't/can't/couldn't feel anything.
13 Can/Do you see a ship over there?
14 I don't thing so; I think he can see.
15 I think there is; I can hear/heard a radio.

**Senses and actions: Can you work it out?**
A

| | | | | | |
|---|---|---|---|---|---|
| 1 b | 2 a | 3 a | 4 b | 5a | 6 b |
| 7 b | 8a | | | | |

B
1 3, 5, 6 2 1, 2, 4, 7

C

| | | | | | |
|---|---|---|---|---|---|
| 1 a | 2 b | 3 a | 4 b | 5 a | 6 b |

**Unit 13 Present perfect and past simple**
1 Drat! I've spilt my wine.
2 I went to Australia in 1982.
3 Oh dear! I've forgotten the phone number!
4 In 1969 they landed on the moon.
5 Ouch! I've broken my leg!
6 Margaret Thatcher was Prime Minister from 1979 to 1990.
7 This is the first time I've driven since my driving test.
8 I'm afraid I haven't skied before.

**Present perfect and past simple: Can you work it out?**
A

| | | | | | |
|---|---|---|---|---|---|
| 1 b | 2 a | 3 a | 4 b | 5 b | 6 a |
| 7 a | 8 b | 9 b | 10 a | 11 a | 12 b |

B

| | |
|---|---|
| 1 present perfect | 4 past simple |
| 2 past simple | 5 present perfect |
| 3 past simple | |

**Unit 14 The passive 1**
1 I'm afraid it's been stolen.
2 I'm afraid it's going to be demolished.
3 I'm afraid it's been burgled.
4 I'm afraid it'll be enlarged.
5 I'm afraid it's being diverted.
6 I'm afraid it's been knocked down.
7 I'm afraid it's thrown away.

**The passive 1: Can you work it out?**
A

| | | | | | |
|---|---|---|---|---|---|
| 1 a | 2 b | 3 b | 4 a | 5 b | 6 a |
| 7 b | 8 a | 9 a | 10 b | | |

B

| | | | | | |
|---|---|---|---|---|---|
| 1 b | 2 a | 3 a | 4 b | 5 a | 6 b |
| 7 a | 8 b | | | | |

**Unit 15 The past 1**

| | |
|---|---|
| 1 had driven/ had been driving | 10 had told |
| | 11 gave |
| 2 could | 12 drank |
| 3 arrived | 13 felt |
| 4 wasn't | 14 fell |
| 5 had | 15 killed |
| 6 came | 16 said |
| 7 was waiting | 17 wasn't |
| 8 didn't look | 18 had confessed |
| 9 saw | 19 had hidden |

**The past 1: Can you work it out?**
A

| | | | | | |
|---|---|---|---|---|---|
| 1 b | 2 a | 3 a | 4 b | 5 b | 6 a |
| 7 a | 8 b | 9 a | 10 b | | |

B

| | |
|---|---|
| 1they had been driving | 3 had worked |
| 2 had been deserted | 4 died |

C

| | |
|---|---|
| 1 same | 3 different |
| 2 different | 4 same |

D
1 b 2 a

**Unit 16 Conjunctions**
1 ... unless you want to see the sights.
2 ... in case you get lost.
3 ... although many people think they are too crowded.
4 ... unless you want to spend a lot of money.
5 ... as long as you arrive early to avoid the crowds.
6 ... although you will find it very noisy.
7 ... as long as you don't mind a long journey.
8 ... in case you want to buy a lot of presents.

**Unit 17 Getting it right 1**

| | |
|---|---|
| Paragraph 1: | 1 for the wonderful present |
| | 2 because I've lost my voice |
| | 3 I'll be able to speak |
| Paragraph 2: | 4 in Cardiff |
| | 5 I already like Wales |
| | 6 what the differences are |
| | 7 such a lot/so many |
| | 8 which I can see |
| | 9 afraid of making |
| | 10 I'll ever manage |
| Paragraph 3: | 11 I haven't found a job yet |
| | 12 unless I do find one |
| | 13 depend on Gwyn |
| | 14 I had been an import-export |
| Paragraph 4: | 15 are so empty |
| | 16 a policeman stopped me |
| | 17 I should be driving |
| | 18 I could be prosecuted |
| | 19 I will have to pay |
| Paragraph 5: | 20 what happened to you |
| | 21 you had already left |
| | 22 when you can visit |
| Paragraph 6: | 23 in case you didn't |

**Unit 18 Wish 1**

| | |
|---|---|
| 1 had checked | 4 see/will see/have seen |
| 2 had | 5 hadn't come |
| 3 had brought | |

**Unit 19 Modal verbs 3**
1 could/might even have died
2 should have listened
3 should have checked
4 shouldn't go
5 could/might easily have missed
6 would have been
7 would know
8 could learn/would learn
9 should have taken
10 should have told
11 shouldn't have gone out
12 would have been
13 should have known
14 could/might still catch

**Unit 20 Modal verbs 4**
A
1 have gone
2 have lent
3 find/have found
4 have finished
5 have fallen/fall

B
1 would have been
2 could/might have finished
3 should have dug
4 would certainly have finished
5 would/might/could have fallen
6 should have finished
7 could move

**Modal verbs 4: Can you work it out?**
A

| | | | | | |
|---|---|---|---|---|---|
| 1 b | 2 a | 3 b | 4 a | 5 a | 6 b |
| 7 a | 8 b | | | | |

B

| | | | | | |
|---|---|---|---|---|---|
| 1 b | 2 a | 3 a | 4 b | 5 a | 6 b |

C

| | | | | |
|---|---|---|---|---|
| Possible endings: | 1 b | 2 a | 3 a, b | 4 a, b |
| | 5 a | 6 a | 7 b | |

**Unit 21 Substitution words**
1 've got any
2 will/could lend us/you some
3 want to
4 'd prefer that
5 hope not
6 think so
7 phone them
8 have lost it
9 use this
10 teach myself
11 haven't bought one/didn't buy one

**Substitution words: Can you work it out?**
A

| | | |
|---|---|---|
| 1 a ✓ b ✗ c ✓ | 4 a ✓ b ✗ c ✓ | 6 a ✓ b ✓ c ✗ |
| 2 a ✓ b ✓ c ✗ | 5 a ✗ b ✓ c ✓ | 7 a ✓ b ✓ c ✗ |
| 3 a ✓ b ✗ a ✓ | | |

B

1 have some? 2 have one? 3 of myself

**Unit 22 The future 1**
A
1 will be selling
2 will have installed
3 will have appointed
4 will have raised
5 will have solved
6 will be printing

B

| | |
|---|---|
| 1 a) will have taken | b) will be talking |
| 2 a) will be typing | b) will have left |

**The future 1: Can you work it out?**
A

| | | | | | |
|---|---|---|---|---|---|
| 1 b | 2 a | 3 b | 4 b | 5 a | 6 b |

B
*Actions in progress*
... 'll be living in a warmer climate.
... 'll be working as an agriculturalist.
... 'll be living in a comfortable house.

*Actions completed*
... 'll have met the right person.
... 'll have paid back all the money my parents lent me.
... 'll have published the results of my research thesis.

C
1 will have doubled
2 will be feeding
3 will have found
4 will be facing
5 will have contributed

**Unit 23 Used to**
1 ... I can get used to driving on the left.
2 ... I'll never get used to having a tiny kitchen.
3 ... I can't get used to the cold.
4 ... I used to know it well.
5 ... Sarah has got used to/is used to her new school.
6 ... I'm not used to studying/I can't get used to studying.
7 ... I'm not used to giving people orders.
8 ... I used to play football (before my accident).
9 ... I still haven't got used/but I'm still not used to getting up so early.
10 ... I'm not used to being alone.
11 ... I get/I've got used to the keyboard.
12 ... I used to do it/sail a lot when I was at college.

**Used to: Can you work it out?**
A

| | | | | | |
|---|---|---|---|---|---|
| 1 b | 2 a | 3 a | 4 b | 5 b | 6 a |
| 7 a | 8 b | 9 a | 10 b | 11 a | 12 b |

B

| | | | | |
|---|---|---|---|---|
| 1 c | 2 b | 3 a | 4 e | 5 d |

C

| | | | |
|---|---|---|---|
| 1 b | 2 a | 3 d | 4 c |

D

| | |
|---|---|
| used to | + infinitive |
| be used to | + verb-ing |
| be used to | + noun |
| get used to | + verb-ing |
| get used to | + noun |

**Unit 24 Relative clauses 1**
A
1 chemist
2 launderette
3 playground
4 pelican crossing
5 newsagent
6 shop assistant

B

| | | |
|---|---|---|
| 1 a ✗ b ✓ c ✗ | 3 a ✗ b ✓ c ✗ | 5 a ✗ b ✓ c ✗ |
| 2 a ✓ b ✗ c ✓ | 4 a ✓ b ✓ c ✓ | |

C

1 a) when/which you celebrate
  b) you celebrate
2 a) you don't know
  b) who you don't know
3 a) which wakes you up
  b) that wakes you up
4 a) who doesn't eat meat
5 a) where children play
  b) children play in

**Unit 25 Checking ahead 2**

1b 2a (see units 39, 47)  5a 6b (see units 27, 28, 44)
3a 4b (see units 27, 28, 44)  7b 8a (see units 35, 45)

**Unit 26 Adverbs of time 2**

| | | |
|---|---|---|
| 1 often | 5 just | 9 already |
| 2 since | 6 sometimes | 10 until |
| 3 twice | 7 before | 11 rarely |
| 4 ago | 8 once | 12 yet |

Hidden word: occasionally

**Unit 27 Infinitive and gerund 1**

| | | |
|---|---|---|
| 1 coming | 4 throwing | 6 shouting |
| 2 marrying | 5 to tell | 7 to feed |
| 3 to watch | | |

**Unit 28 Infinitive and gerund 2**

A

| | | |
|---|---|---|
| 1 to light | 4 to teach | 7 going |
| 2 lighting | 5 to lock | 8 to tell |
| 3 teaching | 6 going | |

B

| | | | | | |
|---|---|---|---|---|---|
| 1 b | 2 a | 3 a | 4 b | 5 b | 6 a |
| 7 b | 8 a | 9 a | 10 b | 11 a | 12 b |

**Infinitive and gerund 1 and 2: Can you work it out?**

A

| | | | | | |
|---|---|---|---|---|---|
| 1 a | 2 a | 3 b | 4 b | 5 a | 6 a |
| 7 b | | | | | |

B

| | |
|---|---|
| 1 remembered, saw | 5 regretted, told |
| 2 saw, stopped | 6 although she talked |
| 3 stopped, saw | 7 because she couldn't talk |
| 4 told, regretted | |

**Unit 29 Modal verbs 5**

1 b, d, g, k  2 e, h, j  3 a, c, f, i

B

| | | | | | |
|---|---|---|---|---|---|
| 1 b | 2 a | 3 d | 4 e | 5 c | 6 h |
| 7 f | 8 g | 9 j | 10 i | 11k | |

**Modal Verbs 5: Can you work it out?**

A

| | |
|---|---|
| 1 a) might/could | c) will |
| b) won't | d) might/could |
| 2 a) could/might | c) can't |
| b) could/might | d) must |
| 3 a) can't have | c) might have/could have |
| b) might have/could have | d) must have |

B

| | |
|---|---|
| 1 could, might | 5 must have |
| 2 must | 6 can't have, couldn't have |
| 3 can't, couldn't | 7 could have, might have |
| 4 could, might | |

**Unit 30 Countable and uncountable 2**

A

| *uncountable* | *countable* |
|---|---|
| 2 countryside | 1 teeth |
| 3 accommodation | 4 mice |
| 5 secrecy | 7 sheep |
| 6 advice | 10 people |
| 8 travel | |
| 9 furniture | |
| 11 information | |
| 12 work | |

B

| *always singular* | *always plural* |
|---|---|
| the news | the police |
| each (of them) | scissors |
| politics | the poor |
| either (of them) | both (of them) |
| everyone | all (of them) |
| maths | trousers |

**Unit 31 The passive 2**

1 a  2 b  3 a  4 b

**Unit 32 The passive 3**

1 she was examined (by a doctor)
2 he renovated it
3 they are painted

**The passive 2 and 3: Can you work it out?**

A

| | |
|---|---|
| 4 It (the film) | 7 The film |
| 5 Ms O'Neill's costumes | 8 It (the film) |
| 6 Her dresses | |

B

4 It was directed by Luca Lopez and produced by Pablo Mendes.
5 Ms O'Neill's costumes are said to be outstanding.
6 Her dresses were specially designed by Gocci.
7 The film has already been nominated for several awards.
8 —

C

| | | |
|---|---|---|
| 1 pasta | 5 China | 9 Italy |
| 2 Italy | 6 He | 10 it |
| 3 Marco Polo | 7 discovery | 11 Italy |
| 4 it | 8 pasta | 12 China |

**Unit 33 Articles**

A

| | | |
|---|---|---|
| 1 a violent film | 5 the violence | 9 films |
| 2 violent films | 6 the quality | 10 children |
| 3 Violence | 7 the film | |
| 4 life | 8 a film | |

B

Unemployment is one of the most important problems in the world today. It affects all countries: not only South America, Africa and Asia, but also Europe and the United States too. And it is not just a modern problem either; it has been with us for centuries. Unemployment destroys people's lives, it breaks up the family and it makes society poor. The question is: what can we do about it?

**Articles: Can you work it out?**

A

The true sentences are: 2, 3, 5, 6

B

a 5 b 6 c 3 d 2

C

1 b 2 a 3 a 4 b 5 b 6 a
7 a 8 b

**Unit 34 Modal verbs 6**

1 heard/could hear
2 couldn't phone
3 decided
4 could swim/swam
5 managed to swim
6 climbed
7 couldn't start
8 found
9 began
10 managed to row

**Modal verbs 6: Can you work it out?**

A

1 b 2 a 3 b 4 a 5 a 6 b
7 a 8 b

B

1 managed to, was able to
2 could, was able to
3 didn't manage to, couldn't, wasn't able to
4 couldn't, wasn't able to

C

1 b 2 a 3 a 4 b

**Unit 35 Reporting**

A

1 She ordered the dog to sit.
2 The waiter suggested the customer should have fish.
3 She warned the boy to be careful.
4 He invited his girlfriend to go to a party.
5 He told his daughter to tidy her room.
6 The manager reminded her secretary to ring Ms Adams.

**Reporting: Can you work it out?**

A

1 wanted, asked, told, persuaded, reminded
2 agreed, thought, insisted, said, suggested

B

1 advised
2 said
3 persuaded
4 thought

C

what previous experience they had
if they had previous experience
if they had taken a university course
what their last job had been
what university course they had taken
if they had liked their last job

D

1 correct
2 I asked them if they had worked for a publishing company before.
3 I asked what their previous job had been.
4 I also wanted to know what they would do in the future.
5 I advised some candidates to come back when they had more experience.
6 I asked/told the best two to come back for a second interview.

**Unit 36 Past and present**

A

1 did you notice
2 are you shaving
3 have you been waiting
4 have you done
5 were you driving
6 do you meet

B

1 was living
2 realised
3 had been
4 was climbing
5 saw
6 had been drawn
7 was
8 recognised
9 was
10 began
11 have been haunting/have haunted
12 used to sacrifice/sacrificed

**Unit 37 Getting it right 2**

1 ... writing back so quickly.
... I hope to get one soon.
... the person who lives ...
2 ... I really wish she didn't need to work so much.
... I often can't stop thinking ...
... I just remember eating ...
... I used to do at home.
... I wish I hadn't come here ...
... Gwyneth could have found a job ...
... I'm enjoying myself here on the whole ...
...I'm still not used to hearing the language.
3 I really like the countryside ...
... I went for a long walk ...
... eventually I got home ...
4 ... finding a job./finding work.
... the woman whose husband ...
... some good advice.
She has suggested that I put ...
I really wish I could find ...
... economics isn't really my field.
5 ... perhaps I have left it in Denmark/perhaps I left it in Denmark ...
I'll probably be looking for a job ...
6 Please remember to get in touch ...

**Unit 38 Look, look like, look as if**

A

1 She looks
2 She looks as if
3 She looks
4 She looks as if
5 She looks like
6 She looks like
7 She looks
8 She looks as if

B

1 sounds like
2 She sounds as if
3 She sounds like
4 She sounds as if
5 She sounds
6 She sounds as if
7 She sounds like
8 She sounds

**Look, look like, look as if: Can you work it out?**

A

1d ice
2f (old) socks
3b applause/clapping
4e runner
5a old woman

B

| | |
|---|---|
| 1 like | 3 — |
| 2 like | 4 as if/as though |

C

| | | |
|---|---|---|
| 1 smells like | 3 sounds like | 5 looks as if/as though |
| 2 tastes | 4 sounds as if/as though | |

**Unit 39 Relative clauses 2**

1 , which is the first building in the village,
2 where/inwhich I had spent my childhood
3 , (which is) when my father died
4 which wasn't surprising in the circumstances,
5 (which) the council was building past the village
6 which was going to go through his favourite wood
7 , who had parked the car and walked back,
8 , which is when I realised how crazy the whole thing was
9 , who/whom I trust completely,
10 , which she had passed on the way down,
11 , which really would go through my father's favourite wood,
12 , which is why I am opposing the plan to build it

**Relative clauses 2: Can you work it out?**

A

| | | | | | |
|---|---|---|---|---|---|
| 1 b | 2 a | 3 a | 4 b | 5 b | 6 a |

B

| | |
|---|---|
| 1 defining | 5 defining |
| 2 non-defining | 6 non-defining |
| 3 defining | 7 defining |
| 4 non-defining | 8 non-defining |

**Unit 40 Wish 2**

A

1 he hadn't said he didn't want to stay.
he hadn't broken a very expensive vase.
2 he wouldn't play with his food.
he would do what I say.
3 he didn't miss his parents.
he could dress himself.

B

1 you would play by yourself.
2 you hadn't lost your favourite toy.
3 you could read.
4 you wouldn't sing at 6.00 every morning.
5 I hadn't shouted at you last week.
6 you hadn't torn my favourite book.
7 you wouldn't chase the dog.
8 you had some other children to play with.
9 you were old enough to understand how difficult you are.

**Wish 2: Can you work it out?**

A

| | | | | | |
|---|---|---|---|---|---|
| 1 a | 2 b | 3 b | 4 a | 5 b | 6 a |

B

| | | | |
|---|---|---|---|
| 7 b | 8 a | 9 a | 10 b |

C

1 3 Please buy me a walkman!
5 Please get your hair cut!
9 Please listen to me!
2 8, 10
3 6, 7

D

| | | |
|---|---|---|
| 1 b | 2 c | 3 a |

**Unit 41 Simple and continuous**

| | |
|---|---|
| 1 stood | 10 tasted |
| 2 looked | 11 was keeping |
| 3 kept | 12 was having |
| 4 was having | 13 was holding |
| 5 weighed | 14 was tasting |
| 6 was being | 15 was standing |
| 7 held | 16 was looking |
| 8 was weighing | 17 had |
| 9 was making | |

**Simple and continuous: Can you work it out?**

A

| | | | | | |
|---|---|---|---|---|---|
| 1 b | 2 a | 3 b | 4 a | 5 a | 6b |
| 7 a | 8b | | | | |

B

| | | | | | |
|---|---|---|---|---|---|
| 1 b | 2 a | 3 a | 4 b | 5 b | 6 a |
| 7 a | 8 b | | | | |

**Unit 42 If sentences 1**

| | |
|---|---|
| 1 hadn't gone to America | 6 had told |
| 2 caught the 10 o'clock bus | 7 had come in |
| 3 had had a gun | 8 hadn't invented |
| 4 had thrown the receipt away | 9 had stopped |
| 5 didn't study hard | |

**If sentences 1: Can you work it out?**

A

Clauses which are possibly true are: 3, 4, 7, 8
Clauses which are definitely not true are: 1, 2, 5, 6, 9

B

| | | |
|---|---|---|
| 1 c | 2 a | 3 b |

C

1 If the captain sent a radio signal before the ship sank
2 If Les is here now
3 If Les had been here now
4 If Sarah said anything to your boss while you were away
5 If Sarah had said anything to your boss while you were away
6 If Ali bought the tickets when the box office first opened
7 If Ali had bought the tickets when the box office first opened
8 If I'd had any more food
9 If have any more food

**Unit 43 Prepositions 2**

A

| | |
|---|---|
| 1 on | 4 in |
| 2 through | 5 with |
| 3 with | |

B

1 you (drink) through
2 you (find) words in
3 you (keep) money in
4 you (borrow) books from
5 you (hang) coats on
6 you (open) bottles with

**Unit 44 Infinitive and gerund 3**

A

| | |
|---|---|
| 1 arrange | 7 manage |
| 2 avoid | 8 miss |
| 3 choose | 9 plan |
| 4 consider | 10 practise |
| 5 decide | 11 refuse |
| 6 deny | 12 recall |

B

| | |
|---|---|
| 1 to stay | 6 attacking |
| 2 to get | 7 to give |
| 3 to have | 8 seeing |
| 4 to meet | 9 dropping |
| 5 stealing | |

**Unit 45 The past 2**

1 was carrying, died
2 gave, promised
3 were going to see, heard
4 was wearing, saw
5 was going to send, died
6 told, had written
7 sent, had been killed
8 took, met

**The past 2: Can you work it out?**

A

1 were climbing (a hill).
2 had just got up.
3 were eating (a picnic).
4 was going to have a shower.
5 finished.

B

a 2 b 1 and 3 c 5 d 4

**Unit 46 Adverbs of time 3**

A

| | |
|---|---|
| 1 ago | 6 yet |
| 2 when | 7 for |
| 3 since | 8 while |
| 4 never | 9 still |
| 5 ever | |

Hidden word: The trainer

B

| | |
|---|---|
| 1 over | 7 whenever |
| 2 ago | 8 ages |
| 3 long | 9 these days |
| 4 moment | 10 time |
| 5 sooner or later | 11 present |
| 6 every now and then | 12 during |

**Unit 47 Relative clauses 3**

A

| | | | | | |
|---|---|---|---|---|---|
| 1 a | 2 b | 3 b | 4 a | 5 b | 6 a |
| 7 b | 8 a | 9 b | 10 a | 11 b | 12 a |

B

1 (that/which) she couldn't reach.
2 whose name she can never remember.
3 , (which are) the largest mammals in the world,

**Unit 48 Articles and countable and uncountable nouns**

1 If you need help, please ask for assistance
2 All you need is love
3 Hair wanted
4 Please leave cameras at the desk
5 Roadworks ahead
6 Will all personnel please report to the main office.
7 Advice Centre
8 Collect your luggage here
9 Now showing: *Journey to the Centre of the Earth*
10 If you have a complaint, please ask to see the manager.
11 Beauty is in the eye of the beholder
12 Please turn off the light.
13 The sun rises in the east and sets in the west
14 Travel agent
15 Take a card, any card
16 Please ring the bell for service
17 Please shut the door
18 English spoken here.
19 There is a time and a place for all things
20 Foreign money not accepted
21 The End

**Unit 49 The future 2**

1 Actually, I'm meeting an old friend there.
2 Not long, I'm/'ll be leaving on Sunday.
3 Yes, I'm going to visit the colleges.
4 In that case, I'll go there too.
5 I'm afraid I'll be working (in the university library) at three o'clock.
6 Let's see. Shall I ring you at 6.00 pm on Thursday?
7 In that case, I think I'll buy one.
8 If it's good, shall I get you one?
9 OK. I'll ring you on Thursday.

**Unit 50 If sentences 2**

1 If I had had some change I would have rung.
2 Don't worry. If I need anything I'll help myself.
3 I wouldn't have brought them if I hadn't wanted to.
4 I'll certainly come if I have time.
5 Don't worry. If I don't remember I'll ring you to ask again/I can always ring if I can't remember.
6 Well, I think I would (like to) go there if I had enough money.
7 I'm not sure. She'll come if she (has) got a plane ticket.
8 Yes, I'd still be/have been waiting if I hadn't caught it.
9 I would go to bed if I weren't/wasn't waiting for a phone call.

**Unit 51 Getting it right 3**

| | |
|---|---|
| 1 one | 8 should |
| 2 are | 9 were |
| 3 the | 10 Who did it? |
| 4 to tell | 11 will be able to |
| 5 should | 12 will be taught |
| 6 to answer | 13 could be |
| 7 brown | |

# Index

**All entries refer to unit numbers not page numbers.**